Lynching and Murder in the Deep South

Other titles in this series:

Lynching and Murder in the Deep South

Lucent Library of Black History

Michael V. Uschan

LUCENT BOOKS

An imprint of Thomson Gale, a part of The Thomson Corporation

THOMSON

GALE

™

Detroit • New York • San Francisco • New Haven, Conn. • Waterville, Maine • London

In memory of James Cameron, founder of America's Black Holocaust Museum in Milwaukee, Wisconsin, and a survivor of a lynching in Marion, Indiana, in 1930.

© 2007 Thomson Gale, a part of The Thomson Corporation.

Thomson and Star Logo are trademarks and Gale and Lucent Books are registered trademarks used herein under license.

For more information, contact
Lucent Books
27500 Drake Rd.
Farmington Hills, MI 48331-3535
Or you can visit our Internet site at http://www.gale.com

LIBRARY OF CONGRESS CATALOGING-IN-PUBLICATION DATA

Uschan, Michael V., 1948-
     Lynching and murder in the deep South / by Michael V. Uschan.
          p. cm. — (Lucent library of Black history)
     Includes bibliographical references and index.
     ISBN-13: 978-1-59018-845-3 (hard cover : alk. paper)
     ISBN-10: 1-59018-845-4 (hard cover : alk. paper) 1. Lynching—Southern States—History—Juvenile literature. 2. African Americans—Violence against—Southern States—History—Juvenile literature. 3. Southern States—Race relations—History—Juvenile literature. I. Title. II. Series.
     HV6464.U73 2006
     364.1'34—dc22
                                                                                    2005037807

Printed in the United States of America

Contents

Foreword

It has been more than five hundred years since Africans were first brought to the New World in shackles, and over 140 years since slavery was formally abolished in the United States. Over 50 years have passed since the fallacy of "separate but equal" was obliterated in the American courts, and some forty years since the watershed Civil Rights Act of 1965 guaranteed the rights and liberties of all Americans, especially those of color. Over time, these changes have become celebrated landmarks in American history. In the twenty-first century, African American men and women are politicians, judges, diplomats, professors, deans, doctors, artists, athletes, business owners, and home owners. For many, the scars of the past have melted away in the opportunities that have been found in contemporary society. Observers such as Peter N. Kirsanow, who sits on the U.S. Commission of Civil Rights, point to these accomplishments and conclude, "The growing black middle class may be viewed as proof that most of the civil rights battles have been won."

In spite of these legal victories, however, prejudice and inequality have persisted in American society. In 2003, African Americans comprised just 12 percent of the nation's population, yet accounted for 44 percent of its prison inmates and 24 percent of its poor. Racially motivated hate crimes continue to appear on the pages of major newspapers in many American cities. Furthermore, many African Americans still experience either overt or muted racism in their daily lives. A 1996 study undertaken by Professor Nancy Krieger of the Harvard School of Public Health, for example, found that 80 percent of the African American participants reported having experienced racial discrimination in one or more settings, including at work or school, applying for housing and medical care, from the police or in the courts, and on the street or in a public setting.

It is for these reasons that many believe the struggle for racial equality and justice is far from over. These episodes of discrimi-

nation threaten to shatter the illusion that America has completely overcome its racist past, causing many black Americans to
become increasingly frustrated and confused. Scholar and writer
Ellis Cose has described this splintered state in the following way:
"I have done everything I was supposed to do. I have stayed out
of trouble with the law, gone to the right schools, and worked
myself nearly to death. What more do they want? Why in God's
name won't they accept me as a full human being?" For Cose and
others, the struggle for equality and justice has yet to be fully
achieved.

In many subtle yet important ways the traumatic experiences
of slavery and segregation continue to inform the way race is dis-
cussed and experienced in the twenty-first century. Indeed, it is
possible that America will always grapple with the fallout from its
distressing past. Ulric Haynes, dean of the Hofstra University
School of Business has said, "Perhaps race will always matter,
given the historical circumstances under which we came to this
country." But studying this past and understanding how it con-
tributes to present-day dialogues about race and history in America is a critical component of contemporary education. To this
end, the Lucent Library of Black History offers a thorough look at
the experiences that have shaped the black community and the
American people as a whole. Annotated bibliographies provide
readers with ideas for further research, while fully documented
primary and secondary source quotations enhance the text. Each
book in the series explores a different episode of black history;
together they provide students with a wealth of information as
well as launching points for further study and discussion.

Introduction

The Tools of Racial Terrorism

On August 18, 1901, in Pierce City, Missouri, Gisella Wild taught a Sunday school class and attended church with her mother. That was the last time she was ever seen alive. Searchers later found Wild's body, dumped in a ditch bordering some railroad tracks. She had been brutally slain, her throat cut. When a witness claimed he had seen an African American man near the tracks shortly before Wild was believed to have been killed, a manhunt began.

The arrest the next day of thirty-two-year-old Will Godley ignited a wave of violence. A mob numbering more than one thousand angry whites broke into the Pierce City Jail and took Godley from his cell. The lynchers then hung Godley from an awning of the Lawrence Hotel and riddled his suspended body with bullets. The mob then went to the home of his grandfather, French Godley, shot him to death, and set fire to his house. Pete Hampton, an elderly friend of Godley's, died in the blaze. Members of the mob continued their rampage by burning down other homes in the city's black section and attacking anyone they met. The black victims in Pierce City were killed even though it was never proved that Godley or another black had killed Wild. The violence terrified three hundred black residents so much that they fled the city and never returned.

Godley, his grandfather, and Hampton were among the 105 black lynching victims in the United States in 1901. Mark Twain, one of America's greatest writers, wrote a powerful essay that condemned the Pierce City incident. Twain also expressed his sorrow that the violence had tainted the reputation of his home state: "And so Missouri has fallen, that great state! Certain of her children have joined the lynchers, and the smirch is upon the rest of us. That handful of her children have given us a character and labeled us with a name, and to the dwellers in the four quarters of the earth we are 'lynchers,' now, and ever shall be."[1]

The title of Twain's essay—"The United States of Lyncherdom"—was itself a caustic comment on how widespread lynching was at the start of the twentieth century. Lynching was particularly common in the South, however. Indeed, in 1901 90

A political cartoon from the 1870s depicts blacks and their status among whites.

percent of the lynchings that year occurred in states that had been part of the Confederacy during the Civil War.

Part of the reason that lynching was so common in the South was the determination on the part of the region's whites to maintain their dominance over blacks. The North's victory in the Civil War in 1865 put an end to slavery. In the years immediately after the war, the federal government also passed constitutional amendments giving blacks rights they had never had before. Blacks went from being slaves to being U.S. citizens entitled to vote in elections, attend school, and work and live wherever they chose.

Federal laws and constitutional amendments did little to erase the belief that blacks were racially inferior to white people. In the South white supremacists formed groups like the Ku Klux Klan (KKK) that used violence to deny blacks their new rights and keep them subservient to whites. Members of the KKK and other southerners beat up and even killed blacks who tried to exercise these new rights. An African American who tried to vote, for example, did so at the risk of his life.

The perpetrators of these lynchings often tried to justify them by claiming that their victims had committed some sort of crime. Rarely had the black victim actually done anything illegal. Usually, the victim's only "offense" was that his or her skin was black. African American historian Carroll R. Gibbs claims lynching was generally designed to arouse the maximum in fear—to use violence as a means of controlling black people. Said Gibbs: "Lynching is the ultimate form of terrorism. There is an old African American proverb that says that the ax forgets, but the tree remembers. Black folks knew this was always terrorism, even though the larger [white] community tried to make it seem like law and order."[2]

In the closing decades of the nineteenth century, lynching reached epidemic proportions. In 1882 the Tuskegee Institute began compiling statistics on how widespread lynching had become. Between 1882 and 1968, when the last case that was officially classified as a lynching occurred, 3,445 black people were lynched in the United States. The vast majority of these crimes occurred in the Deep South. Mississippi had 539 lynchings, the most of any state, while Georgia recorded 492, Texas

Masked horsemen ride away from a hanging body after a lynching.

352, Louisiana 335, and Alabama 299. To put that figure into perspective, two or three blacks were lynched every week in the South during the late nineteenth century and early twentieth century. Lynchings peaked in 1892, when 161 blacks were murdered by lynch mobs.

Lynching, however, was only one of several forms of racial terrorism. Countless other African Americans were killed or severely injured in riots in which white mobs invaded black neighborhoods, shooting or beating blacks they encountered and setting fire to blacks' homes. Such widespread violence sometimes followed a lynching, as happened in Pierce City. However, race riots were sometimes ignited when the local press printed false or greatly exaggerated reports of crimes committed by blacks against whites. One of the worst examples of this phenomenon occurred in September 1906 in Atlanta, Georgia. In a four-day period, several thousand whites rampaged through black districts of the city, killing twenty-five blacks, injuring hundreds of others, and forcing more than a thousand to flee for their lives. The riot was sparked by newspaper stories that contained false claims that blacks were attacking white women.

No One Knows How Many Died

The resulting scars on black Americans' collective psyche proved long lasting. When African American author James Baldwin traveled to the South for the first time in the 1950s, the region's history of white-on-black violence weighed heavily on his mind. When Baldwin saw Georgia's red clay hills from his airplane, a strange idea popped into his mind: "I could not suppress the thought that this earth had acquired its color from the blood [of black victims] that had dripped from these trees."[3] It was a vivid mental image. But it was one based on the reality of the southern blacks' experience.

Chapter One

The Brutality of Lynching and Murder

On May 21, 1917, a black prisoner named Ell Persons was being taken by train from Nashville to Memphis, Tennessee, to stand trial for the slaying of a white teenager, Antoinette Rappel. The trial never took place. When the train arrived in Memphis, members of a waiting mob seized the prisoner from the deputy sheriffs and took him to a prearranged site, where thousands of people had already gathered to witness his death. A *Memphis Press* newspaper story described the crowd that watched him die:

> Fifteen thousand of them—men, women, even little children, and in their midst the black-clothed figure of [Rappel's mother]—cheered as they poured the gasoline on the fiend and struck the match. They fought and screamed and crowded to get a glimpse of him, and the mob closed in and struggled about the fire as the flames flared high and the smoke rolled about their heads. Two of them hacked off his ears as he burned; another tried to cut off a toe but they stopped him.[4]

Even though his death did not result from hanging, the murder of Persons was a lynching. In 1920 the Tuskegee Institute, a private college dedicated to educating African Americans, published its definition of lynching: For a murder to be considered a lynching, "there must be legal evidence that a person has been killed and that he met his death illegally at the hands of a group [a mob] acting under the pretext of service to justice, race, or tradition." The school defined a group as "three or more persons."[5]

How Lynching Began

Lynching was not originally designed as a means of terrorizing African Americans, however. During the American Revolution, a Virginia planter named Charles Lynch and his neighbors took it upon themselves to arrest and punish suspected criminals even

A white murder suspect is about to be hanged in an illustration that depicts an era when all sorts of crimes ended at the hangman's noose.

though they had no legal standing as law officers or judges. They did this because the chaos of the war had made it difficult for local officials to maintain law and order.

In the nineteenth century, this crude form of justice became known as lynch law. People living in frontier areas with no established law enforcement agencies adopted lynch law to curb crime. An article in an 1843 edition of *British and Foreign Review* magazine explained why Americans believed they were justified in employing lynch law: "In a new and thinly peopled country every man feels that he may at any time be called upon to act as his own protector."[6]

Offenses such as murder, rape, or stealing livestock were punishable by death. These executions became known as lynchings, and hanging was the usual means of carrying out the sentence. Often, the participants in the executions were so numerous that they were referred to as lynch mobs.

Most historians believe that until the end of slavery in 1865, more whites than blacks were the victims of lynchings. Historians assert that the majority of blacks in America prior to 1865 were slaves and were too valuable to their owners to be killed if they committed an offense. Only when the slaves were freed, then, was there any motivation for lynching, which quickly became a means of social control.

The Tuskegee Institute noted that lynchings were motivated in part by race and tradition, which meant keeping African Americans subservient. Blacks who tried to vote in elections, learn to read and write, or work in jobs other than those formerly reserved for slaves did so at the risk of their lives.

Southern whites preferred not to acknowledge publicly the underlying motive for lynching, nor did they really even bother trying to justify the practice. In his 1905 book on lynching, James Elbert Cutler noted that racial prejudice was usually cited as the reason for a lynching. An example was the February 22, 1898, murder of Frazier Baker, the black postmaster in Lake City, South Carolina. Resentful that a black man held a government job, a white mob set fire to his home, which also housed the post office. Someone then shot Baker as he fled the burning building. The town newspaper listed "race prejudice" as the reason for the murder. Wrote Cutler: "The probable reason for giving race prejudice as a cause for lynching is that no offense had been committed which was considered worthy of mention as a cause."[7]

A Public Spectacle

Baker's murder was unusual in that only the lynchers who killed him witnessed his death. In contrast, many lynchings were public spectacles viewed by hundreds and even thousands of men, women, and even children. Some historians labeled these killings "public torture lynchings." Historian David Garland explains the elements of this type of lynching:

> The most notorious lynchings that occurred in the USA between 1890 and 1940 involved publicity, crowds, ritual, and abnormal cruelty. Four to five hundred of these "public torture lynchings" took place, most of them in the Deep South [when] crowds began to torture and burn alleged offenders with unprecedented ferocity and public ceremony.[8]

The pattern for such brutality was set on February 1, 1893, with the lynching of Henry Smith in Paris, Texas. Smith was accused of killing three-year-old Myrtle Vance, whose father was a policeman who had often arrested and beaten him. The young girl's death so outraged whites that they decided to make Smith's death memorable as a warning to other blacks not to harm whites. After seizing Smith from officers who were guarding him, lynchers seated him on a large, flat wagon so that everyone could see him as he was taken to the site where he would be lynched.

His death was witnessed by ten thousand people who had traveled there from hundreds of miles away on horseback, in wagons, and on trains. After Smith was placed on a ten-foot-high scaffold (3m) so everyone could watch what was happening, the girl's father and other relatives burned Smith with hot irons; they even poked out his eyes. A newspaper reported that during the torture, which lasted nearly an hour, "Smith screamed, prayed, begged and cursed his torturers."[9] Members of the mob then doused Smith with oil and set him on fire. Afterward, onlookers cut pieces from Smith's charred body as souvenirs and even took his teeth.

Lynching Was Illegal

In 1905 James Elbert Cutler wrote a book in which he stated that Americans should be ashamed that the practice of lynching still existed in the United States. Wrote Cutler:

> It has been said that our country's national crime is lynching. We may be reluctant to admit our peculiarity in this respect and it may seem unpatriotic to do so, but the fact remains that lynching is a criminal practice which is peculiar to the United States. The practice whereby mobs capture individuals suspected of crime, or take them from the officers of the law, and execute them without any [legal] process at law, or break open jails and hang convicted criminals, with impunity, is to be found in no other country of a high degree of civilization. Riots and mob executions take place in other countries, but there is no such frequent administration of what may be termed popular justice which can properly be compared with lynch-law procedure in the United States. The frequency and impunity of lynchings in the United States is justly regarded as a serious and disquieting symptom of American society.

Angered by the lynching of a black rape suspect awaiting trial, rioters storm a courthouse.

James Elbert Cutler, *Lynch-Law: An Investigation into the History of Lynching in the United States.* New York: Longmans, Green, 1905, p. 1.

How the Crowds Gathered

Lynchers wanted huge crowds to witness these displays of brutality. Spectators and the news media were expected to spread the word so the lynchings would serve as a warning to other blacks. The clear message was that a similar fate awaited anyone who threatened the supremacy of whites. Southern newspapers helped draw large crowds to lynchings by printing details of the

A large crowd gathers to witness the lynching of Henry Smith in Texas in 1893.

time and place they were to be held. Those planning these crimes knew that the authorities would not intervene. An example of the mass media's complicity was an article in the October 26, 1934, edition of the *Macon Telegraph*. The story informed readers in Georgia that a mob had seized Claude Neal from jail, where he was being held as a suspect in the death of a white woman named Lola Cannidy, and was going to lynch him at her father's home in Greenwood, Florida. The newspaper included details on where Neal would be lynched and quoted a member of the mob, who declared, "All white folks are invited to the party." [10] Encouraged by such stories, an estimated seven thousand people from several states gathered to watch Neal die. After Neal was severely beaten, a woman killed him by plunging a knife into his heart.

Those who wrote the stories about lynchings made no effort to conceal their racism or bias. Stories and headlines usually referred to the lynching victim as a "brute," "unspeakable wretch," or a "negro desperado." The newspapers' editorials praised lynchings as a way to control blacks who otherwise would be a danger to whites. Moreover, reporters and editors often admitted they enjoyed attending lynchings. On October 10, 1911, a local newspaper editor was present in Honea Path, South Carolina, when Willis Jackson was hung upside down from a tree and shot numerous times, allegedly as punishment for attacking a white child. In his story in the *Intelligencer*, Victor B. Chesire admitted he "went out to see the fun without the least objection to being a party to help lynch the brute."[11]

Many people who attended lynchings brought cameras so they could photograph the event. Professional photographers also went to lynchings so they could take pictures and sell the photos as souvenirs. For several decades, images of hung men or burned, disfigured bodies were printed on postcards and many people sent the gruesome photos to friends and relatives. It was not until 1908 that the federal government made it illegal to send such gruesome images through the U.S. mail.

Members of a lynch mob pose next to the body of a man who was hanged and then set on fire in Missouri.

The Point of Brutality

The brutality depicted in such photos was, of course, deliberate. That fact eluded people living in the North, who were appalled by the viciousness of southern lynch mobs. When Richard Coleman was tortured and burned to death in Maysville, Kentucky, on December 6, 1899, the *New York Times* condemned the lynching's cruelty. The

---

Lynching Postcards

For many decades, southerners sent postcards featuring pictures of lynching victims to friends and members of their family. In an article David Garland wrote about lynching in 2005 for *Law & Society Review*, he describes some of the postcards and the messages people wrote on them:

> One postcard, with a photograph showing a large crowd in downtown Dallas, is addressed to "Dr. J.W.F. Williams, Lafayette, Christian County, Kentucky" and reads: "Well John, This is a token of a great day we had in Dallas, March 3rd [1910], a negro was hung for an assault on a three year old girl. I saw this on my noon hour. I was very much in the bunch. You can see the Negro hanging on a telephone pole." Another, carrying an image of the charred, barely recognizable, corpse of Jesse Washington, suspended from a utility pole in Robinson, Texas, was sent by Joe Meyers to his parents in May 1916. The message reads: "This is the Barbecue we had last night my picture is to the left with a cross over it your son Joe."

This picture of Jesse Washington's body was put on a postcard in 1916.

David Garland, "Penal Excess and Surplus Meaning: Public Torture Lynchings in Twentieth-Century America," *Law & Society Review*, December 2005, p. 810.

Times article noted that what the mob did to Coleman was "an outrage so terrible and so shameful that it can only be explained as an outbreak of popular delirium. [He died] amid demonstrations of brutality and barbarity of the most revolting character."[12]

Some lynchings, however, were so gruesome that even southerners had trouble stomaching them. One example was a lynching that was dubbed the "Waco Horror." On May 15, 1916, in Waco, Texas, Jesse Washington was found guilty of murdering Lucy Fryer, the wife of a farmer who had employed him. When the guilty verdict was read, whites seized him and took him to city hall for a public lynching. While Washington was being dragged to his death, angry whites kicked, stabbed, and beat him. Before a crowd of fifteen thousand people, lynchers poured oil on Washington and set him ablaze. Afterward, lynchers dragged his burned body through city streets. The violence was so shocking that the *Waco Times-Herald* claimed, "Such a demonstration as of people gone mad was never heard before."[13]

Even women were not safe from the savagery of lynching. On February 7, 1904, a mob in Dodsville, Mississippi, burned to death Luther Holbert, who was accused of killing his employer, James Eastland. When they captured Holbert, the lynch mob also took his wife, even though there was no evidence linking her to the murder. A story in the Vicksburg *Evening Post* detailed what the mob did to the couple: "When the two negroes were captured, they were tied to trees and while [wood was collected to burn them] they were forced to suffer the most fiendish tortures."[14] The torture included cutting off the captives' fingers.

Despite the brutality, some observers seemed to consider lynchings a form of entertainment. This attitude was apparent in a lynching that occurred indoors in April 1911 in Livermore, Kentucky. The victim, Will Porter, was arrested and charged with shooting a white man in a barroom brawl. When it was discovered that the sheriff was hiding Porter in a local theater, a white lynch mob decided to make his death a ghoulish stage show. The perpetrators tied Porter to a pole on the stage and then sold fifty men tickets that entitled them to shoot Porter from their theater seats. An article in the *New York Times* reported that "of about 200 shots fired, nearly half entered the body of the black man and the remainder tore to shreds [stage] scenery."[15]

Murder on a Massive Scale

Lynchings such as the one in which Porter died resulted in the death of an individual or, occasionally, several victims. But the imperative to control blacks that motivated lynchings sometimes exploded into mass attacks on entire communities of blacks. When such race riots broke out, the result could be murder on a massive scale. Such was the case on the evening of September 30, 1919, when Phillips County deputy sheriffs went to a rural Arkansas church to break up a meeting of black farmworkers who wanted to organize to fight for better working conditions. The workers, who were armed, refused to disperse. In the fighting that broke out between the two sides, one deputy was killed. Another was wounded in an exchange of gunfire. The sheriff was so full of rage that the blacks had fought back that he issued an order "to hunt Mr. Nigger in his lair."[16] In the three days that followed, about five hundred whites roamed the area, beating and killing blacks they encountered and burning their homes. Although official reports listed the deaths of only five whites and twenty-five blacks, some historians believe as many as two hundred blacks were killed.

The Arkansas incident was one of scores of episodes of mass violence against blacks in the South. In just two years, between the end of the Civil War in 1865 to 1867, hundreds of blacks were killed and thousands more injured in violence in cities such as Charleston, Atlanta, Memphis, and New Orleans. Always, the point was to keep blacks subservient, just as they had been before slavery ended.

A riot that occurred on March 17, 1886, in Carrollton, Mississippi, shows how whites used riots to punish blacks who tried to stand up for the rights that had so recently been extended to them. Ed and Charley Brown, who were black, accused a white man named Jim Lidell Jr. of attempted murder. When they came to court to testify, sixty whites invaded the courthouse and shot them to death along with twenty-one other blacks. The whites killed the blacks because the brothers had dared to accuse a white man of a serious crime.

Once a riot started, whites who participated showed little or no concern who they beat or killed. One of the worst riots began in Atlanta on September 22, 1906, when whites were whipped into a frenzy by newspaper stories that falsely claimed blacks were sexually assaulting white women. Roving groups of whites began attacking any blacks they encountered, and in four days the mobs killed at least twenty-five blacks. During the riot, thirteen-year-old Walter White, who as an adult would investigate lynchings and race riots, saw whites kill a black man. White described the death:

> We saw a lame Negro bootblack [shoe shiner] from Herndon's barber shop pathetically trying to outrun a mob of whites. Less than a hundred yards from us the chase ended. We saw clubs and fists descending to the accompaniment of savage shouting and cursing. Its work done, the mob went after new prey. The body with the withered foot lay dead in a pool of blood on the street.[17]

The worst period of race riots occurred in the summer and fall of 1919, when violence erupted in twenty-six U.S. cities,

Residents of St. Louis, Missouri, sort through the remains of a fire after a race riot in 1917.

Fighting Off Rioters

———————————◼———————————

In September 1906 when Walter White was thirteen years old, at least twenty-five blacks were killed in a race riot in his hometown of Atlanta. White almost became a victim himself of roving white racists. In his autobiography, *A Man Called White*, he describes how he and his father, who were armed, waited tensely as the rioters drew near their home:

A voice [yelled] "That's where that nigger mail carrier [White's father] lives! Let's burn it down! It's too nice for a nigger to live in!" [My father told me] "Son, don't shoot until the first man puts his foot on the lawn and then—don't you miss!" The mob moved toward the lawn. I tried to aim my gun, wondering what it would feel like to kill a man. Suddenly there was a volley of shots. The mob hesitated, stopped. Some friends of my father's had barricaded themselves in a two-story brick building just below our house. It was they who had fired. Some of the mobsmen, still bloodthirsty, shouted, "Let's go get the nigger." Others, afraid now for their safety, held back. Our friends, noting the hesitation, fired another volley. The mob broke and retreated up Houston Street.

Walter White, *A Man Called White*. New York: Arno, 1969, p. 9.

including Charleston, South Carolina, and Washington, D.C. African American poet James Weldon Johnson named this murderous period the "Red Summer" because so many blacks were killed or injured.

Johnson, whose characterization of the riots in 1919 was a fitting commentary on their violence, was also concerned about lynchings. He investigated the lynching of Ell Persons on behalf of the National Association for the Advancement of Colored People (NAACP). The brutality of Persons's death stunned Johnson, who argued that such violence was morally degrading to whites who committed it. Said Johnson: "I tried to balance the sufferings of the miserable victim against the moral degradation of Memphis, and the truth flashed over me that in large measure the race question involves the saving of black America's body and white America's soul."[18]

Chapter Two

Maintaining Social and Racial Order Through Violence

In 1961 when Joseph Holloway was nine years old, his family traveled by car from their home in Los Angeles, California, to Louisiana, where his parents had been born. While driving through a small town in Texas, the Holloways encountered a white lynch mob of about five hundred people. The lynchers had tied their victim to a wheel and set him on fire. When one of the whites saw the Holloway family car, he shouted, "There's some more niggers, let's get them." Holloway's uncle drove away fast enough to escape the danger. But decades later Holloway recalled that the brutal incident has always haunted him: "I've never been back to that place except in my nightmares."[19]

The lynching, Holloway learned, was part of a conscious effort on the part of white racists to enforce the system of segregation that had been part of southern life since the end of the Civil War. Holloway and his family were barred from most hotels, restaurants, and even public bathrooms. Holloway remembers that when he asked why they were treated that way, his uncle told him: "Well, Joe, that's the way things is in the South. This is not Los Angeles, this is the South and that's just

Magazine illustrations from 1871 satirize lynchings and unfair murder trials during the Reconstruction era.

the way things are here. I don't much like them, but there is nothing we can do. Nothing!"[20]

His uncle had not really answered his question. But when Holloway grew up to become a professor of Pan-African Studies at California State University at Northridge, he was able to explain to his students how the lynching that he had witnessed and the segregation that he and his family had experienced were intertwined. The lynching, Holloway came to understand, was one of thousands of violent acts perpetrated to maintain white supremacy.

Re-enslaving Blacks

That supremacy had been threatened as never before in 1865 by the North's victory in the Civil War. The Thirteenth Amendment to the Constitution, passed later that year, had abolished slavery. But Walter White, a black civil rights leader who in the early twentieth century risked his life to investigate lynchings, wrote that southerners showed themselves to be unwilling to accept the end of slavery: "The vast majority of the whites were united in a single cause—to re-enslave the Negro as far as was humanly possible."[21]

To do that, most states of the defeated Confederacy passed what were called Black Codes. These laws prohibited blacks from owning property and voting, restricted where they could live, and limited them to jobs as laborers or servants. Congress tried to nullify the codes by passing the Civil Rights Act of 1866, but President Andrew Johnson vetoed the measure. A southerner from Tennessee, Johnson claimed, "This is a country for white men, and by God, as long as I am President, it shall be a government for white men."[22]

Although the bill became law when Congress overrode Johnson's veto, little changed for many blacks. Blacks who dared to object to the continuation of white supremacy were simply killed. Between 1865 and 1868, for example, Texas alone recorded the slayings of one thousand black citizens. A black person could be killed on the flimsiest of pretexts—or for no reason at all. One white man shot a black because he failed to take off his hat when they met; another white man justified shooting a black by saying, "I wanted to thin out the niggers a little."[23]

Underlying this brutal determination to continue white supremacy was the belief white southerners held that they were physically and mentally superior to blacks. This racist viewpoint was even promoted by some whites who had opposed slavery. For example, the antislavery activist Hinton R. Helper claimed in 1867 that "the Negro is a fellow of many natural defects and deformities [including] a thick skull and a booby brain."[24]

Reconstruction Era Violence

Congress sought to protect blacks with two constitutional amendments. The Fourteenth Amendment granted blacks citizenship and equal protection under the law with whites, and the Fifteenth Amendment specifically guaranteed blacks the right to vote. To quiet ongoing disorder in the South, Congress in 1867 also passed the Reconstruction Acts, which gave the U.S. government civil and military control over the former Confederate states. These acts also included provisions to help the former slaves make new lives by establishing schools and by giving them land to farm.

For a time it seemed that white supremacy was finally at an end. During Reconstruction, which lasted until 1877, southern blacks

Beating a Black State Legislator

■

After the Civil War Abram Colby, a former slave, was elected to the Georgia legislature. In 1872 Colby testified before a congressional committee how members of the Ku Klux Klan on October 29, 1869, beat him up to stop him from voting in an election a few days away. Colby, who continued with his political career despite being severely beaten, describes the incident:

> [The Klansmen] broke my door open, took me out of bed, took me to the woods and whipped me three hours or more and left me for dead. They said to me, "Do you think you will ever vote [again]?" I said, "If there was an election tomorrow, I would vote." They set in and whipped me a thousand licks more, with sticks and straps that had buckles on the ends of them. Some are first class men in our town. One is a lawyer, one a doctor, and some are farmers. They had their pistols and they took me in my night-clothes and carried me from home. They hit me five thousand blows. . . . My little daughter begged them not to carry me away. They drew up a gun and actually frightened her to death. [That] was the part that grieves me the most.

A cartoon from 1874 illustrates a black family being terrorized by members of white supremacy groups.

Quoted in Dorothy Sterling, *The Trouble They Seen: Black People Tell the Story of Reconstruction*. Garden City, NY: Doubleday, 1976, p. 374.

enjoyed rights previously reserved for whites. They could vote, and many were elected to public office, including the U.S. House of Representatives and U.S. Senate. In southern states, black state legislators helped write laws that erased the Black Codes.

But even though federal troops helped ensure that blacks got the rights to which they were entitled, the new citizens were still not safe from harm. Organizations like the KKK, the White League, and the Knights of the White Camellia were created to oppose Reconstruction and maintain white supremacy. Their members attacked blacks who tried to exercise the rights Congress had granted them. Northern whites the federal government sent south to oversee Reconstruction were also beaten and sometimes lynched.

Most of the violent incidents occurred in nighttime raids on the homes or businesses of blacks by mounted riders from groups like the KKK. They would beat or whip blacks, burn their homes, and destroy their property as a warning that they must continue to obey whites. The armed men wore robes and hoods to disguise their identity. The violence became so bad in Calhoun, Georgia,

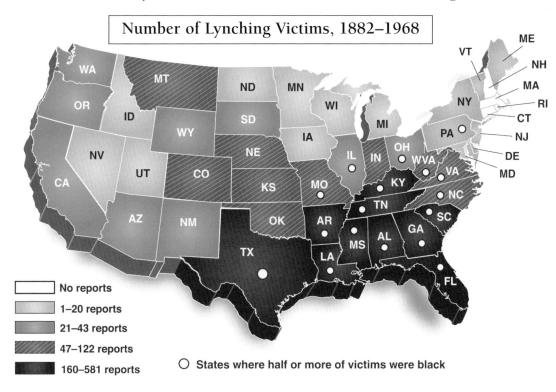

Number of Lynching Victims, 1882–1968

No reports

1–20 reports

21–43 reports

47–122 reports

160–581 reports

○ States where half or more of victims were black

in 1867 that a group of blacks drafted a letter to military authorities in which they asked for protection. They asserted: "There has been houses broken open, windows smashed and doors broken down in the dead hours of the night, men rushing in, cursing and swearing and discharging their pistols inside the house. Men have been knocked down and unmercifully beaten and yet the authorities do not notice it at all."[25]

The tactic night riders used most often to intimidate their victims was whipping, because this had been the punishment used

During a nighttime raid, a black man is dragged down the street by a white mob carrying guns and torches.

most often against slaves. The whippings, which sometimes killed the victim, were a brutal reminder to blacks that even though slavery had ended, whites still had power over them. In 1872 Harriet Hernandes of Spartanburg, South Carolina, told a congressional delegation investigating the violence how prevalent whipping was in her area: "It is all of them [her neighbors], mighty near. Ben Phillips and his wife and daughter; Sam Foster; and Moses Eaves, they killed him—I could not begin to tell all."[26]

The Rise of Jim Crow

The plight of blacks became worse in 1877. Republican president Rutherford B. Hayes, who had been narrowly elected in 1876, needed southern votes in Congress to pass legislation. Hayes, in order to mollify southerners, agreed to withdraw U.S. troops from the former Confederate states and end Reconstruction. Southern states once again had the power to govern themselves. Without federal oversight, their legislatures quickly passed bills that eliminated the rights that blacks had briefly enjoyed. The new laws prohibited blacks from voting, barred them from holding office, and segregated them in every aspect of daily life.

The resulting system of segregation that reduced blacks to second- class citizens became known as Jim Crow, after a fictional character in minstrel shows that was a demeaning caricature of African Americans. In the Jim Crow South, blacks could not attend school with whites, travel on train cars with whites, or enter stores, restaurants, and other businesses that were reserved for whites. An example of this segregation is what happened in 1898 to Susie King Baker Taylor when she traveled from Boston to Louisiana to see her dying son. Taylor had paid for a first-class ticket. But when she reached Cincinnati, she was forced to move to a Jim Crow car because the train would soon be entering segregated southern states. Taylor, who had served as a nurse in the Civil War, balked at sitting in the car because it was never kept as clean as those reserved for whites and smoking was allowed. But in her autobiography, Taylor wrote that she realized she had no choice but to endure the filthy conditions: "I went to this car and on entering it all my courage failed me. I had ridden in many coaches, but I was never in such as these. I wanted to return home again, but I thought of my sick boy. I

Black and white passengers in 1943 board buses outside of a segregated waiting room in Tennessee.

said, 'Well, others ride in these cars and I must do likewise,' and tried to be resigned."[27]

Riding in uncomfortable conditions was just one of many indignities blacks suffered under Jim Crow. There was also the rigid etiquette they had to follow in dealing with whites. Although blacks always had to address white men and women as "sir" or "ma'am," whites routinely replied using derogatory nicknames, such as "Auntie" or "boy." A black person could not shake hands with a white because a handshake was traditionally only offered to an equal. Blacks could never show anger toward whites, even if they insulted or cheated them, and had to defer to whites in virtually any situation. For example, if a white and a black approached each other on a sidewalk, the black had to step aside into the street, for a black brushing up against a white person was unthinkable. Stepping off the sidewalk was mandatory even if the street was muddy or strewn with manure from horses.

The tangle of obligations for African Americans hemmed them in on all sides. W.E.B. Du Bois, an early twentieth-century black civil rights leader, once commented that Jim Crow stripped blacks of all that they had gained after the Civil War. Said Du Bois: "The slave went free; stood a brief moment in the sun; then moved back again toward slavery."[28]

Enforcing Jim Crow

For nearly a century, whites used violence and brutality to force blacks to submit to Jim Crow. Beatings, rape, arson, and violent death awaited blacks who challenged white supremacy. In pursuit of their goal of keeping them under control, whites murdered hundreds of blacks for the slightest offenses. For example, in 1901 whites in Romo, Tennessee, hung to death Ballie Crutchfield because they thought she had helped her brother steal a white woman's purse. And in Pilot Point, Texas, in 1922, two unemployed blacks being held in connection with the theft of a pair of horses were taken from the jail and never seen again. An unsigned note sent to the local newspapers said the two men "got what they had coming" and stated, "Let this be a warning to all nigger loafers. Niggers get a job or leave town."[29]

Blacks who managed to get ahead despite the racism they faced found that success was no protection if they seemed to challenge the status quo. An example of this happened on October 21, 1916, when Anthony P. Crawford went to Abbeville, South Carolina, to sell a load of cotton he had grown. While arguing with the buyer about the price for his cotton, Crawford called him a liar. Crawford was arrested for being disrespectful to a white man but was freed from jail after paying a fifteen dollar fine.

That was not the end of the matter, however. When Crawford went to retrieve his cotton, a mob attacked him because he had sassed a white man. After Crawford fought back and injured one of his assailants with a hammer, the other whites began kicking and stabbing him. The sheriff arrested Crawford again so the mob would not kill him, but later that day the mob angrily broke into the jail and hung Crawford from a tree in a brutal lynching.

No one was ever tried for Crawford's murder. In fact, some white townspeople argued that his lynching was justified, not just because he had been disrespectful to whites, but because he was relatively wealthy. A letter to the *Abbeville Press and Banner* newspaper from a local resident claimed, "He was getting rich, for a negro, and he was insolent along with it."[30] Moreover, the manager of a local store suggested that the death of a black person was of little consequence among the whites in the area: "When a nigger gets impudent we stretch him out and paddle him a bit."[31]

Throughout the South during the early decades of the twentieth century, lynching was never far from the region's black residents. In 1919, a year in which there were seventy-six lynchings of blacks, a Savannah, Georgia, newspaper reported that African Americans were more frightened than ever of indiscriminate white violence: "There is scarcely a Negro mother who does not live in dread and fear that her husband or son may come in unfriendly contact with some white person so as to bring the lynchers, which may result in the wiring out of her entire family."[32]

Having served one's country was no help if one fell afoul of local whites. Among the blacks murdered in 1919 were a dozen African Americans who had served in the U.S. Army during World War I. When these war veterans came home, some whites worried that these men might see equal treatment as something they were due in return for fighting for their country. To remind anyone who might be harboring such ideas of just where they stood, whites attacked and lynched black soldiers. Some were still wearing their uniforms when they died.

What white supremacists were most determined to prevent was African Americans—veterans or not—exercising the right to vote that the Fifteenth Amendment had guaranteed them. Whites knew that if blacks could vote, they would elect black candidates who promised to eliminate Jim Crow. So it was that people like

The Blacks They Targeted

Frederick Douglass, who was born a slave in 1817 but became one of the most influential early advocates of civil rights for African Americans, was a fierce opponent of lynching. In 1892 in an article titled "Lynch Law in the South," Douglass wrote that whites lynched many blacks because they were successful:

> The distressing circumstances in this revival of lynch law in different parts of the South is, that it shows that prejudice and hatred have increased in bitterness with the increasing interval between the time of slavery and now. The resistance met by the negro is to me evidence that he is making progress. The negro meets no resistance when on a downward course. It is only when he rises in wealth, intelligence, and manly character that he brings upon himself the heavy hand of persecution. . . . When the negro is degraded and ignorant he conforms to a popular standard of what a negro should be. When he shakes off his rags and wretchedness and presumes to be a man, and a man among men, he contradicts the popular standard and becomes an offense to his surroundings.

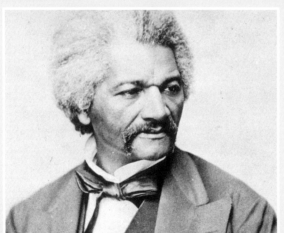

Frederick Douglass was a forceful voice against lynching.

Quoted in Anne P. Rice, ed., *Witnessing Lynching: American Writers Respond.* New Brunswick, NJ: Rutgers University Press, 2003, p. 41.

Harry T. Moore of Mims, Florida, who in 1915 angered whites by trying to register black voters, became targets of the lynchers. On December 25 Moore and his wife, Harriette, were killed when a bomb—a new lynching weapon—exploded at their home. Their deaths illustrated something Moore had once said: "Freedom

In 1949 Alabama, the Ku Klux Klan bombed this house, which once belonged to a black family.

never depends on people. It is always bought with a price."[33] Moore and his wife were just the first of many casualties in an effort that eventually succeeded in the 1960s and 1970s, in gaining African Americans a voice in the governing of their nation.

The Fight Goes On

Although the number of racially motivated murders and lynchings gradually declined in the last four decades of the twentieth century, some say that the racism that fueled that violence still exists. For example on June 7, 1998, James Byrd Jr. was killed in Texas by three whites who beat him unconscious, chained him to a car, and then dragged him to death. When the three were tried in 1999, Jasper County prosecuting attorney Pat Hardy compared Byrd's murder to a lynching and described it in those terms: "Three robed riders came straight out of hell. . . . Instead of a rope, they used a chain, and instead of horses, they had a pick-up truck."[34]

Chapter Three

The Face of Hatred: The Perpetrators of Violence

On December 6, 1899, twenty-year-old Richard Coleman was scheduled to go on trial in Maysville, Kentucky, for killing the wife of a wealthy white farmer who employed him as a laborer. Before the court proceeding could begin, members of a mob seized him from sheriffs' deputies and took him to a pre-arranged lynching site, where they tied Coleman to a tree, piled brush and wood around his feet, and set him on fire. James Lashbrook, the slain woman's husband, lit the blaze that killed Coleman. A story on the lynching that appeared the next day in the *New York World* newspaper described the many different types of people who witnessed his death: "The population of the whole city and country for miles around, church men and church women, professional and business men of eminence, people of distinguished ancestry, formed the mob, and not a single regret for the horrible tragedy can be heard tonight from one end of the town to the other."[35]

Coleman's lynching illustrates an important truth about southern lynching—that the people who killed blacks and those who gathered to watch the brutal slayings came from all

Confederate soldiers attack black Union soldiers during the Civil War. Many southerners refused to treat blacks as equals after the war.

classes of people. Lynch mobs were composed not only of poor, illiterate whites—a class of people sometimes dismissively referred to as "poor white trash"—but also educated and respected members of the communities in which such violence occurred. These mobs included women and children as well as men. The June 1914 edition of the *Crisis*, the magazine published by the NAACP, described the crowd of several thousand people, which earlier that year had witnessed the lynching of Thomas Brooks in Fayette County, Tennessee: "People in automobiles and carriages came from miles around to view the corpse dangling from the end of a rope. Women and children were there by the score. At a number of country schools the day's routine was delayed until boy and girl pupils could get back from viewing the lynched man."[36]

A shared determination to maintain white supremacy allowed people of varied social and economic classes to participate in lynchings, even if it was only as spectators. But at the time the era of racially motivated lynching began, those who murdered blacks were drawn together by another shared emotion—anger over having lost the Civil War.

The Ku Klux Klan

When the war ended on April 9, 1865, those who had fought for the Confederacy were embittered over their defeat. Those who had owned slaves were also furious that the U.S. government had deprived them of their property. Most objectionable of all for whites—whether they had owned slaves or not—was the prospect of having to accept blacks as equals. In this climate of anger and resentment, former soldiers formed groups like the KKK, Knights of the White Camellia, Knights of the Rising Sun, and the Pale Faces, the objective being to oppose the federal government's effort to help former slaves build new lives as freedmen and freedwomen. The targets of these organizations were not just blacks, but white northerners the federal government had appointed to help govern the newly readmitted states during Reconstruction.

Journalist Carl Schurz, a German immigrant who had fought for the Union in the Civil War, noted that the defeated southerners seemed unprepared to accept the new reality:

> The incorrigibles still indulge in the swagger which was so customary [during] the war and still hope for a time when the Southern confederacy will achieve its independence. This class consists mostly of young men, and comprise the loiterers of the towns and the idlers of the country. They persecute Union men and Negroes wherever they can do so with impunity."[37]

Of the white supremacist groups, the most potent was the KKK, which was founded in 1866 in Pulaski, Tennessee, by six former Confederate soldiers. It soon had members in every southern state. The Klan soon found a leader in Nathan Bedford Forrest, a former slave trader who had become one of the Civil War's greatest cavalry officers. Forrest was delighted when he first heard about the new group: "That's a good thing; that's a damn good thing. We can use that to keep the niggers in their place."[38] Forrest was elected the Klan's first Grand Wizard—its top official.

Like other KKK members, Forrest believed whites must keep blacks subservient and that violence to achieve that objective was justified. Clad in white robes and hoods to disguise themselves, Klansmen targeted blacks who attempted to vote or attend school, or who demanded that they be treated equally with whites. KKK members beat and killed blacks irrespective of gender. In addition, black women were subject to rape. In July 1868 General W.P. Carlin, assigned by the federal government to help govern Tennessee, reported on how widespread the KKK violence had become:

> Complaints are continually coming in of outrages committed by the Ku Klux Klan. The colored people are leaving their homes [in rural areas], and are fleeing to towns and large cities for protection. The Ku Klux Klan's organization is so extensive and [their members] so well organized and armed [that] powder and ball is the only thing that will put them down.[39]

In a reign of terror that lasted into the early 1870s, Klansmen also attacked and murdered whites who tried to help former slaves improve their lives, including those who taught in schools serving blacks. Eventually, Klan violence became so extreme that it even appalled Forrest. In 1869 he ordered the KKK to disband, claiming the organization's attacks against blacks were "becoming injurious instead of subservient to the public peace."[40] Although many members initially ignored the request, the number of KKK chapters (known as klaverns) gradually declined in the next few decades. However, this decline had less to do with Forrest's attitude and more to do with the Klan's goal of restoring white supremacy, which was largely accomplished after 1877 and the end of Reconstruction.

Passing Hatred on to Children

In 1927 Walter White wrote *Rope and Faggot*, a book based on his experience investigating lynchings for the National Association for the Advancement of Colored People. White was shocked to learn that southerners allowed children to view such violence. White recounts a conversation he had with three white children who had watched five blacks burned to death. Because White had light skin, blue eyes, and blond hair, the children talked openly to him about the murders they had witnessed a few days earlier. Wrote White:

> Three shining-eyed, healthy, cleanly children, headed for school, approached me. As I neared them, the eldest, a ruddy-cheeked girl of nine or ten, asked if I was going to the place where "the niggers" had been killed. I told her I might stop and see the spot. [White was headed there to collect facts for his investigation.] Animatedly, almost as joyously as though the memory were of Christmas morning or the circus, she told me, her slightly younger companions interjecting a word here and there or nodding vigorous assent, of "the fun we had burning the niggers." One need not be a sentimentalist to feel that such warping of the minds of Southern children is by far the worst aspect of lynching.

A young boy attends a lynching in Georgia in 1915.

Walter White, *Rope and Faggot: A Biography of Judge Lynch*. New York: Arno and the *New York Times*, 1969, p. 3.

Hundreds of Owensboro, Kentucky residents gather to witness a hanging of an accused murderer in 1936.

"Best People of the County"

The decline of the Klan as an organized movement, however, did not mean that blacks in the South were any safer from attack. Lynchings actually increased during the remainder of the nineteenth century. What changed was the backgrounds of those perpetrating the violence. Although many former Confederate soldiers still participated in violence targeting blacks, the motives of those instigating the attacks gradually changed. Now, in addition to being motivated by ideas of racial superiority, attackers carried with them a jealousy of their victims.

In the late nineteenth and early twentieth centuries, most blacks lived in rural areas, where they either farmed small plots of land or worked for whites who owned large farms. Yale University historian Robert A. Gibson claims that economic and social factors were both in play:

> Lynchings occurred most commonly in the smaller towns and isolated rural communities of the South where people were poor, mostly illiterate, and where there was a noticeable lack of wholesome community recreation. The people who composed mobs in such neighborhoods were usually small land holders, tenant farmers and common laborers, whose economic status was very similar to that of the Negro. They frequently found Black men economic competitors and bitterly resented any Negro progress.[41]

Certainly, the lynching of Anthony Crawford, the cotton farmer who argued with a white broker over the selling price of cotton, was in part based on the precarious financial position of some of his assailants. In commenting on Crawford's death, a South Carolina newspaper noted that whites were jealous of Crawford because he owned a farm valued at almost twenty thousand dollars. The paper claimed that sum was "more than most white farmers are worth down here [and] the cracker [a derogatory term for a rural southerner] can't stand it."[42]

It was not only such lower-class whites, however, who participated in the systematic killing of blacks. In describing the lynching of Elmo Curl on June 12, 1910, in Mastodon, Mississippi, a local newspaper declared that the town's best citizens had helped make the illegal execution "a most orderly affair." Said the paper: "[The lynching] was conducted by the bankers, lawyers, farmers and merchants of the county. The best people of the county [Panola County], as good as there are anywhere, simply met there and hanged Curl without a sign of rowdyism. There was no drinking, no shooting, no yelling, and not even any loud talking."[43]

Among the respected citizens who participated in lynchings were politicians, some of whom stood to win votes from other racist whites for their actions. In 1908 William Van Amberg Sullivan, a former U.S. senator from Mississippi, was quoted in a newspaper story boasting about his involvement in the brutal hanging of a black man. "I led the mob which lynched Nelse Patton and I am proud of it," Sullivan proclaimed. "I directed every movement of the mob and I did everything I could to see that he was lynched."[44] And on October 10, 1911, South Carolina state legislator Joshua W. Ashleigh led a mob that hung Willis Jackson in Honea Path, a community he represented.

So it was that what united the perpetrators of racial violence was the belief that because they were white, they were superior to blacks. In 1928 civil rights leader Walter White attributed white violence to "the belief that any white man, no matter how inept, criminal, or depraved, is infinitely superior to the 'least Negro who ever lived.'"[45]

Justifications for Violence

This racist belief was supported and spread by writers of the day. Blacks were commonly portrayed in newspaper stories, books, and magazines as inferior, immoral, innately savage, and therefore a menace to white people. Typical of this racial stereotyping is the way in which Charles H. Smith described blacks in a book he wrote in the 1890s: "A bad negro is the most horrible creature upon the earth, the most brutal and merciless."[46] In the early twentieth century, racists employed the new mass medium of film to spread these misleading stereotypes about blacks; the 1915 silent film *The Birth of a Nation*, which depicted them as bestial threats to whites, is considered by historians to be particularly notorious in this regard.

The most damaging myth these media portrayals fostered was that black men lusted after white women and would rape them if given the chance. Whites saw preventing sexual contact between black men and white women as being of utmost importance. In 1918 the *Little Rock [AR] Daily News* defended this view when it claimed that it was proper to lynch any black who dared to cast "lustful eyes on [a] white woman" and thus "seek to break down the barrier that has been between the negro and white man for a thousand years."[47] The breaking of this barrier by white men who assaulted black women was not addressed in this article, despite such incidents being commonplace.

A Film Classic Praises the Ku Klux Klan

The Birth of a Nation is the most controversial U.S. movie ever made. The 1915 silent film based on Thomas Dixon's novel *The Clansman* was set during the period of the Civil War and Reconstruction. The movie and book both twisted the facts of these historical events to glorify the Ku Klux Klan and justify lynching blacks. Although the film became a box-office hit and is considered an important movie because of technical innovations it featured like night photography and close-ups, its racist content led to protests in northern cities. In *The Fiery Cross: The Ku Klux Klan in America*, historian Wyn Craig Wade claims the movie's popularity helped revive interest in the Klan:

> [M]any diehard Yankees were deeply affected by the film. As one said after leaving the theater, "It makes me want to go out and kill the first Negro I see." Others wondered aloud whether their ancestors had fought on the wrong side during the Civil War. A "Ku-Klux fever," similar to that of Reconstruction, was revived in the North [and] the South's response was profound. The Chester [South Carolina] *Semi-Weekly News* pronounced the film "a sacred epic," and for many [southerners] *The Birth of a Nation* was a near-religious experience. . . . In an astonishing few months, Griffith's masterpiece [made many people think] it would be a good idea to revive the Ku Klux Klan.

Pictured is a promotional poster for *The Birth of a Nation.*

Wyn Craig Wade, *The Fiery Cross: The Ku Klux Klan in America.* New York: Simon and Schuster, 1987, pp. 138–39.

A crowd surrounds two lynching victims in the 1930s. Lynchings were sometimes spurred by interracial relationships.

Certainly, the idea that black men found white women irresistible was a powerful one. Data that the Tuskegee Institute compiled from 1882 to 1952 showed that 19.2 percent of lynching victims had been accused of rape. This charge would be leveled even in cases of consensual sex, and some black men were lynched expressly for being involved in interracial love affairs. A story in the *Memphis Commercial Appeal* on January 14, 1922, reported that a mob had lynched a black man in Florence, South Carolina, for being "intimate with a white woman." But in a letter found in his pocket addressed to "Dearest Ed," the woman had written: "It is too bad that we cannot be together always. My love for you is greater than you can imagine."[48] The woman had to flee the area because she feared other whites would also harm her for violating the interracial sexual taboo.

The belief that black men were a sexual threat to southern white women created such powerful emotions of fear, anger, and loathing that whites were willing to condone any amount of violence to prevent such contact. On August 12, 1897, in Georgia, Rebecca Latimer Felton addressed a group of women on the subject. She said, "If it takes lynching to protect women from drunken ravening, human beasts, then I say lynch a few thousand a week if it becomes necessary."[49]

The threat the whites imagined blacks posed was more than sexual, however. An example of how fears about blacks could escalate into multiple murders occurred on May 16, 1918, in Valdosta, Georgia, when Sidney Johnson shot to death Hampton Smith, the white farmer who employed him as a laborer. Smith's death so enraged local whites that over the next week they killed nine other blacks they encountered while searching for Johnson. None of the nine had been involved in Smith's murder, but a local claimed that their deaths were necessary to teach other blacks a lesson: "It's a matter of safety—we gotta show niggers that they mustn't touch a white man, no matter how lowdown and ornery he is."[50] Johnson himself was eventually shot to death in a gun battle and became the tenth black killed in retribution for the death of one white man.

The depth of the attitude that killing blacks was an acceptable means of protecting whites sometimes surprised even southern authorities. During the time that William J. Northern was governor of Georgia, from 1890 to 1894, scores of Georgia blacks were brutally killed. In 1911, when Northern conducted a survey of the attitudes Georgia citizens had about such violence, the findings bothered him. Said Northern: "I was amazed to find scores and hundreds of men who believed the Negro to be a brute, without responsibility to God, and his slaughter nothing more than the killing of a dog."[51]

The conviction that equated killing a black person with killing an animal was shared by most southerners. Thus, when southern whites did kill blacks, their friends, family, and neighbors did not think they had done anything wrong.

At the Hands of Persons Unknown

Still, those who committed such crimes did not publicize their involvement, and local officials and newspapers cooperated. When a black was lynched, newspaper stories and official reports routinely noted simply that the victim had died "at the hands of persons unknown." Almost never was the assailant unknown, though. Members of lynch mobs rarely bothered to conceal their identities, and in the small communities where most lynchings occurred, it was easy for local residents to know who they were. Lynchers did not have to fear being charged if they were recognized, because white southerners were generally unwilling to punish other whites for crimes committed against blacks.

An example of this was the lynching of Richard Coleman on December 6, 1899, in Maysville, Kentucky. Coleman had been accused of killing a white woman, but before he could be tried, he was taken from jail and burned to death. No one was charged

Courtroom spectators cheer the acquittal of lynchers in South Carolina in 1946.

in his death, even though everyone locally knew who had been responsible. James Lashbrook, the victim's husband, admitted to a *New York World* newspaper reporter that he had ignited the fire and was willing to be punished. The newspaper quoted him as saying, "I did as I thought right, and I will stand for all that may follow." But after talking to Lashbrook following the lynching, the judge ordered him released. The judge explained his decision, saying, "Lashbrook has my sympathy."[52]

The reason many southerners—even public officials—did not think lynchers should be prosecuted, was that they considered lynching a legitimate form of social control. For example, Henry Lowry was burned to death in Nodena, Arkansas, on January 26, 1921, because of allegations that he had murdered two whites. Although Mississippi County sheriff Dwight H. Blackwood could have stopped the slaying, he did nothing, because local residents backed the killing. Said Blackwood: "Nearly every man, woman and child in our county wanted the negro lynched."[53]

"Always in Season"

The attitudes that southern whites had for nearly a century after the Civil War on lynching or killing blacks meant that the lives of southern blacks were constantly in danger. Black men and women knew that in the eyes of many whites, their lives had less value than those of animals. This is how a black man who grew up in Mississippi in the 1930s described what it was like: "In those days it was 'Kill a mule, buy another. Kill a nigger, hire another.' They had to have a [hunting] license to kill anything but a nigger. We was always in season."[54]

Chapter Four

The Effort to End Lynching

One main reason that lynching and other forms of violence against blacks became so common in the South was that the federal government did little to stop them. It took the efforts of civil rights organizations and a few brave individuals to awaken America's conscience before lynching as a widely accepted practice came to an end.

In the South state and local authorities made little or no effort against lynchings, and even the federal government was of little help. On July 26, 1918, President Woodrow Wilson issued a forceful appeal to end lynching. Wilson urged "all who revere America and wish to keep her name without stain or reproach [to] make an end to this disgraceful evil. It cannot live where the community does not countenance it."[55] Lynchings, however, increased from thirty-six in 1917 to sixty in 1918 and seventy-six in 1919, a year when victims included a dozen returning World War I soldiers.

The historical record suggests that Wilson did not speak because he was outraged over this illegal practice or felt compassion for its victims. Instead, his concern was that lynching was hurting the nation's image abroad. Moreover, Wilson never sought legislation that would have given the federal government the power to punish lynchers. Wilson was not the only president, however, who failed to try to stop lynching. Furthermore, Congress never took the step of actually passing legislation that specifically prohibited the murderous practice.

The Black Response to Lynching

In the absence of any effective official protection, African Americans had to fend for themselves. During the late nineteenth and early twentieth centuries, this meant ignoring the daily insults and abuses that whites directed at them. Blacks had to display a subservient or at least respectful attitude toward whites they encountered; any other response could result in horrific consequences, not just for themselves but for an entire community.

This facade of acceptance became a crucial survival tactic that black parents taught their children. Charles Gratton grew up in Birmingham, Alabama, during the 1930s. He remembers how his mother lectured him once on how to shield himself from white wrath when he went to the store for groceries: "Son, if you pass

Members of the National Association for the Advancement of Colored People in Great Britain protest lynching in the United States.

Rape and Lynching

■

Historian Philip Dray claims that many racists exploited fears southerners had of sex between blacks and whites to justify lynching. In his book *At the Hands of Persons Unknown: The Lynching of Black America*, Dray credits anti-lynching activist Ida B. Wells-Barnett, herself an African American, with first exposing how some people used this fear to make southerners accept the brutality of lynching. Writes Dray:

> [She] was one of the first people in America to perceive that the talk of chivalry and beastlike blacks ravishing white girls was largely fallacious and that such ideas were being used to help maintain a permanent hysteria to legitimize lynching, as it reinforced the notion that the races must be kept separate at all costs. What was particularly insidious about this mythology was that, by using as taboo a subject as inter-racial sex and as ubiquitous a fear as "race pollution," it tended to push more moderate whites, even if they disapproved of lynching, to accept it as necessary.

Ida B. Wells-Barnett was a journalist and anti-lynching activist.

Philip Dray, *At the Hands of Persons Unknown: The Lynching of Black America.* New York: Random House, 2002, p. 64.

any white people on your way, you get off the sidewalk. Give them the sidewalk. You know, you move over. Don't challenge white people."[56] When Georgia Sutton was a child in New Bern, North Carolina, her mother taught her another facet of this survival tactic—how to conceal her true feelings about the whites she encountered even when she did not like them. Said Sutton:

My mother told me nobody ever knows what goes through your head. She used to say, "That lady I work for is foolish enough to believe that I really like her," she said. "I'm not thinking about her one way or the other. Just pay me what she owes me." And I learned, too, that I could smile [insincerely] on the outside.[57]

Eventually some blacks decided to stop playing this game. One of the most prominent of these individuals was W.E.B. Du Bois, a civil rights activist who believed that blacks had to stand up to whites. In 1911 after a lynch mob in Pennsylvania had burned a black man to death, Du Bois counseled blacks to start resisting lynchers. Du Bois wrote, "If we are to die, in God's name let us not perish like bales of hay."[58]

A Woman Fights Lynching

Du Bois, however, was hardly the first African American to rise up in protest. One of the first blacks who risked her life to end such violence was Ida B. Wells. Born New Year's Day, 1863, in Holly Spring, Mississippi, this daughter of slaves grew up to use her talents as a writer and speaker to fight lynching for more than four decades.

In the late nineteenth century as part owner of *Free Speech*, a Memphis newspaper, Wells began writing about injustices done to blacks. She soon became the nation's most vocal opponent of lynching. But a series of stories that she wrote on one lynching nearly got her killed. On March 9, 1892, a mob seized three black businessmen from the Memphis jail and shot them to death. The men had been arrested after defending themselves with guns from whites who were trying to destroy their grocery store. The whites had been sent by a white grocer who was angry that he was losing business to the blacks.

Wells was so upset that she advised blacks to leave a city "which will neither protect our lives and property [yet] takes us out and murders us in cold blood when accused by white persons."[59] When hundreds of blacks followed her advice, white businesspeople became angry because they had lost so many customers. That article and others she wrote on the incident so angered local whites that on May 27 a mob gathered to

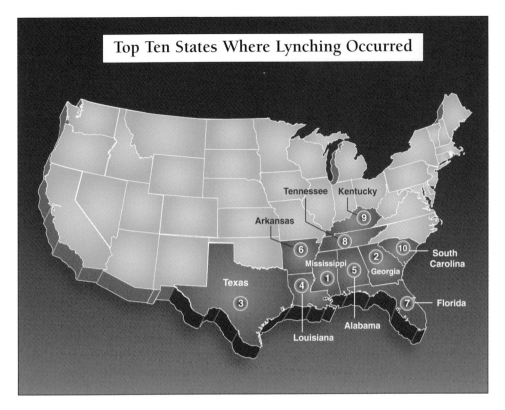

Top Ten States Where Lynching Occurred

destroy the offices in which her newspaper was published. Fortunately for Wells, she was in Philadelphia at the time. Had she been present, she likely would have been lynched, since those who wrecked her property had said they wanted her dead.

Although Wells knew she could never return to Memphis because local whites continued to threaten her life, she refused to quit fighting lynching. "I felt that one had better die fighting against injustice than to die like a dog or a rat in a trap,"[60] she later wrote in her autobiography. Wells moved to Chicago to write for the *Chicago Conservator*, the city's first black newspaper. She eventually married its founder, Ferdinand L. Barnett, and changed her last name to Wells-Barnett.

Wells-Barnett continued to campaign throughout the United States to end lynching. Her outrage over the lyching of two blacks during race riots in Springfield, Illinois, in August 1908 led her and other blacks and whites concerned with such violence to gather in New York in May 1909. During the two-day conference, they founded the NAACP.

The new group, which was composed of whites and blacks, had a much wider purpose than ending lynching; its aim was to help blacks secure their civil rights and to shield them from the effects of racism. But in a memorable speech on the second day of the conference, Wells-Barnett convinced the new organization that an important way to accomplish those goals was to put an end to lynching. She argued, "No other nation, civilized or savage, burns its criminals. Only under the Stars and Stripes is the human holocaust possible."[61]

The *Crisis*

One way the NAACP fought lynching was by publicizing its horrors in its magazine, the *Crisis*. W.E.B. Du Bois edited this journal, which dealt with many issues of particular concern to blacks. In 1919 the group also published *Thirty Years of Lynching in the United States, 1889–1918*, a book that included a state-by-state list of the 2,650 black and 745 white persons who had been lynched in that time period and detailed accounts of one hundred lynchings. It was the most comprehensive lynching publication ever written, and it helped increase public awareness outside the South of how severe the problem was.

The NAACP also began investigating individual lynchings and other forms of racial violence. Their top operative was Walter White, who in 1918 began collecting information on lynchings and race riots. Although he was an African American, his light skin, fair hair, and blue eyes allowed him to pass as white. He was thus in a position to interview white southerners and get their perspective on the violence. He even talked to people who admitted they had killed blacks.

White's work was dangerous; many whites he encountered during his investigations would have killed him had they discovered that he was black. In fact, while probing a race riot that occurred in Elaine, Arkansas, in September 1919, White was nearly lynched himself when local whites learned he was black. He escaped only because a black resident warned him after learning that whites had found out his secret and wanted to kill him. White realized just how much danger he had been in after he boarded a train to leave town and began talking to the train conductor. White recalled that conversation, in which the conductor told him he was going to miss some excitement:

> "Why Mister, you're leaving just when the fun is going to start! There's a damned yaller [light-skinned] nigger down here passing for white and the boys are going to have some fun with him." I asked him the nature of the fun. "Wal, when they get through with him," he explained grimly, "he won't pass for white no more."[62]

The increased exposure that the NAACP gave to such racial violence led to the formation of other groups opposed to it, such as the Anti-Lynching Crusaders and the Commission on Interracial Cooperation (CIC).

Women Oppose Lynching

The CIC was formed in 1919 by white Christian ministers Will Alexander of Tennessee and Willis Weatherford of Texas. In its effort to help blacks and whites live together in peace, the CIC targeted the Klan and in 1921 helped initiate a congressional investigation of the racist organization. In 1930, a year in which lynchings nearly tripled to twenty from seven in 1929, the CIC decided to ask white southern women to help it fight lynching. The CIC wanted their support because women had shown how effective they could be in fighting for a cause a decade earlier by helping to pass the Nineteenth Amendment to the U.S. Constitution, which gave women the right to vote in elections.

The appeal was answered in Texas by Jessie Daniel Ames, who already chaired the Texas Interracial Commission, a group that opposed racism. On November 1, 1930, Ames met in Atlanta with two dozen white women from eight states to found the Association of Southern Women for the Prevention of Lynching. One reason Ames acted was her anger over the May 1930 lynching of George Hughes in Sherman, Texas. Although Hughes had been burned to death for supposedly sexually assaulting a white woman, reports on the lynching indicated the charge was false and that Hughes had been killed because he had argued with his white boss over wages.

Most southerners accepted at face value the myth that black men desired white women so much that they would rape them if they had the chance. But in Atlanta, Ames noted that allegations of blacks raping whites were usually based on rumor and that they were all too often unfairly used to justify murder: "Public opinion has accepted too easily the claim of lynchers and mobsters that they were acting solely in defense of womanhood." Ames declared that southern women had decided they could "no longer remain silent in the face of this crime done in their name."[63]

The fact that white southern women would stand up for black men and try to deny racists one of their major justifications for lynching was a powerful statement that stunned many people. But it made so many southerners angry that the CIC's members often encountered hostility when they investigated violence or spoke out against lynching. Said Ames: "Women went into communities where there had been a lynching. Many of the people

Treason or Rightful Protest?

———————————■———————————

Ida B. Wells-Barnett was nearly arrested in 1917 for distributing anti-lynching buttons. In her autobiography, *Crusade for Justice*, she explains how two U.S. Secret Service agents visited her office in Chicago. They claimed that giving out the buttons hurt the nation's reputation by publicizing lynching, which was condemned by other countries, and that she could be arrested for treason if she continued doing it. When they argued that other blacks did not protest lynching, this is how she responded:

> I said, "Maybe not. They don't know any better or they are afraid
> of losing their whole skins. As for myself I don't care. I'd rather go
> down in history as one lone Negro who dared to tell the govern-
> ment that it had done a dastardly thing than to save my skin by
> taking back what I have said. I would consider it an honor to
> spend whatever years are necessary in prison as the one member
> of the race who protested, rather than to be with all the
> 11,999,999 Negroes who didn't have to go to prison because they
> kept their mouths shut."

Ida B. Wells, *Crusade for Justice: The Autobiography of Ida B. Wells.* Chicago: University of Chicago Press, 1992, p. 52.

Opponents of lynching meet in Texas in 1950 to discuss legislation that would outlaw the practice.

were surly, belligerent. Women were by no means safe. They knew of the constant dangers and didn't forget to pray."[64]

The Drive for Federal Anti-Lynching Legislation

One way the women fought lynching was to back legislative measures in Congress to end it. The reason anti-lynching advocates believed a federal law was needed was that most southern politicians and law enforcement officials were racists themselves and were therefore not apt to protect African Americans. Southern officers of the law rarely tried to stop whites from lynching blacks, and sometimes they even cooperated with the lynchers. On June 26, 1919, for example, John Hartfield was lynched in Ellisville, Mississippi, for allegedly assaulting a white woman. He was killed after the sheriff who had arrested him willingly turned him over to the mob, even though the sheriff knew they were going to kill him.

When a black was lynched or murdered, law officials rarely bothered to arrest anyone, even though they knew the identities of the people involved. And even on the rare occasions when charges were filed, all-white juries almost always found the defendant innocent. This happened in 1931 in Atlanta after Dennis Hubert, a student at Morehouse College, was shot to death for allegedly making an insulting remark to a white woman in a city park. Although his white assailant confessed to killing Hubert, a white jury found him innocent.

The problem of seeking justice for black victims of violence can be seen in what happened in July 1902 in De Kalb County, Tennessee. After a man was charged in the lynching of a black man, the *Chattanooga Times* on July 27 reported that it had been impossible to select a jury because so many local residents had been involved in his death. The paper reported that court officials had interviewed more than 350 potential jurors but had "found every man in the lot disqualified—probably having themselves aided in the affair."[65] No one was ever tried in the case, and in January 1903, when two more men were arrested in the lynching, a mob of thirty masked men freed them from jail.

The first federal bill that would have forced states to prosecute lynchers was introduced in January 1901 by Representative George White of North Carolina. White had been born a slave, and violence targeted at blacks was of special interest to him. In a speech to Congress on January 29, 1901, White urged an end to lynching: "This evil peculiar to America, yes, to the United States, must be met somehow, some day."[66]

Congress never brought White's proposed bill up for a vote. In all, over two hundred bills were introduced in the twentieth century to make lynching a federal crime. They all failed because powerful southerners in Congress opposed them. Among these failed bills was one introduced in 1935 by Senators Edward Costigan of Colorado and Robert F. Wagner of New York. The bill would have made it a crime for law enforcement officials to fail to punish lynchers. Costigan argued that "no man can be permitted to usurp the combined functions of judge, jury and executioner on his fellow men."[67]

The Result of Congressional Inaction

Costigan's and Wagner's bill was not the first such attempt. Indeed, one of the strongest campaigns to secure an anti-lynching bill occurred in 1922 to win passage of the Dyer Anti-Lynching Bill, which made it a crime for law enforcement officials not to punish lynchers. Mary B. Talbert, who was president of the National Association of Colored Women as well as the Anti-Lynching Crusaders, helped create an effective advertising campaign to win support for the measure. In November 1922 the Crusaders placed ads in

"Strange Fruit"

◼

The song "Strange Fruit" is one of the most powerful anti-lynching statements ever made. Abel Meeropol, a Jewish schoolteacher from New York, originally wrote the song's lyrics as a poem because, as he explains, "I hate lynching and I hate injustice and I hate the people who perpetuate it." He took the poem to legendary blues singer Billie Holiday, who teamed with Sonny White to turn it into a song. "Strange Fruit" became one of Holiday's signature tunes. She first sang it in public in January 1939 at Cafe Society, a New York nightclub. In *Strange Fruit: Billie Holiday, Cafe Society, and an Early Cry for Civil Rights* by David Margolick, Holiday admits that

she was worried when she finished singing it for the first time because the crowd showed no reaction: "There wasn't even a patter of applause when I finished. Then a lone person began to clap nervously. Then suddenly everybody was clapping." People who listened had probably been shocked by the song's bitter, powerful lyrics about lynching. The song begins with the line "Southern trees bear a strange fruit." The "fruit" referred to the hanging bodies of lynched blacks and was one of several powerful images describing lynching.

Quoted in David Margolick, *Strange Fruit: Billie Holiday, Cafe Society, and an Early Cry for Civil Rights.* Philadelphia: Running, 2000, p. 37.

Billie Holiday sang "Strange Fruit," an anti-lynching song.

newspapers around the country. They were headlined "THE SHAME OF AMERICA" and asked readers, "Do you know that the <u>United</u> <u>States</u> is the <u>Only</u> <u>Land</u> <u>on</u> <u>Earth</u> where human beings are *BURNED AT THE STAKE?*"[68]

Despite the powerful ads and speeches that people like Talbert made in many cities around the nation, Congress rejected the measure. On December 13, 1922, black poet James Weldon Johnson noted that in just a few weeks since the Senate had killed the Dyer bill, four more blacks had been lynched in the South. In a letter that he sent to every senator, Johnson blamed them for the deaths: "This outbreak of barbarism, anarchy and degenerate bestiality and the blood of the victims rest upon the heads of those Southern senators who have obstructed even the discussion of the measure designed to remedy this very condition."[69]

It would be decades before lynching could be said to have ended. The civil rights movement would finally result in African Americans gaining the equality to which they were entitled. But it would take the sacrifices of many brave men and women who gave their lives to secure those rights.

Chapter Five

Violence During the Civil Rights Era

On January 2, 1954, the headline over a *Washington Post* editorial boldly proclaimed the "End of Lynching." The editorial said the Tuskegee Institute, the black college that had tracked lynching since 1882, had reported that 1953 was the second straight year without a lynching. The newspaper proudly claimed that "at least for the present the blot that has so long stained the American record and poisoned the relations between the white and colored races has been lifted."[70] Although this lynch-free period continued through 1954, there were three lynchings the next year. There would be four more lynchings in years to come. Not until 1968 could those who study racial violence say that the century-long era of lynching had ended.

The decline in lynchings did not mean that southern whites motivated by racism quit killing blacks. In the late 1950s and early 1960s, as the civil rights movement gathered momentum, members of groups like the resurgent KKK continued to use violence against blacks. White supremacists beat and bullied thousands of blacks for daring to demand equal rights and killed scores of victims with a variety of weapons, including guns and bombs. Although these murders did not fall within the narrow definition of a lynching, they were committed for the same reason—to frighten blacks into accepting an inferior status.

One of the most infamous incidents was the September 15, 1963, bombing of the Sixteenth Street Baptist Church in Birmingham, Alabama. Three days after the bombing killed four young girls, KKK leader Charles Conley Lynch praised the attack in remarks before a large crowd of whites in Saint Augustine, Florida: "We're all better off. I believe in violence, all the violence it takes either to scare [blacks] out of the country or to have 'em all six feet under!"[71]

Emmett Till and Rosa Parks

The civil rights movement that the KKK leader opposed so vehemently was, in a way, touched off by a lynching. One of the lynchings recorded in 1955 was the brutal slaying of fourteen-year-old Emmett Till, a Chicago youth visiting his great-uncle in Money, Mississippi. On August 24 Till entered Bryant's Grocery and Meat Market to buy some refreshments. When Till left, he reportedly whistled flirtatiously at Carolyn Bryant, the white store clerk. Although Till had not known it, in the racist South this harmless gesture toward a white woman was considered a deadly insult. In the early morning hours of August 28, two white men abducted Till from his uncle's home. He was never again seen alive. The teenager was found on August 31 in the Talla-hatchie River, a 125-pound (56 kg) electric fan tied to his neck with barbed wire to keep his body submerged. A postmortem examination revealed that after brutally beating him, the kidnappers had shot Till to death with a .45 caliber pistol.

Roy Wilkins, then the executive director of the NAACP, claimed Till's death was another example of white violence designed to keep blacks subservient. Said Wilkins: "Mississippi has decided to maintain white supremacy by murdering children. The killers of the boy feel free to lynch because there is, in the entire state, no restraining influence of decency."[72]

Till's death shocked the nation. It especially angered southern blacks, among them Rosa Parks, a forty-two-year-old seamstress who lived in Montgomery, Alabama. Parks had wept after seeing

A man examines the fan that had been tied around Emmett Till's neck with barbed wire.

pictures of the beaten youth's body in *Jet* magazine. Parks later said that it was the memory of Till's brutal murder that a few months later helped motivate her to take an historic stand for her own civil rights.

On December 1 Parks was riding a crowded bus in Montgomery when the driver told her to give up her seat and move further back so a white man could sit down. When Parks refused because she believed she had a right to her seat after having purchased a ticket, she was arrested. Years later, Parks recalled what had been going through her mind that day: "We [had finally] reached the point where we [blacks] simply had to take action. I thought of Emmett Till and I couldn't go back."[73] Her arrest sparked the Montgomery bus boycott, a dramatic protest which

The Emmett Till Murder

◼

Emmett Till, a fourteen-year-old black Chicago youth, was murdered near Money, Mississippi, on August 28, 1955. Although an all-white jury on September 23 found J.W. Milam and Roy Bryant innocent of killing Till, they later admitted to author William Bradford Huie that they had killed him and even explained how they did it. This description of Till's murder is from a magazine story Huie wrote:

Milam: "Take off your clothes."

Slowly, Bobo [Till's nickname] pulled off his shoes, his socks. He stood up, unbuttoned his shirt, dropped his pants, his shorts.

He stood there naked.

It was Sunday morning, a little before 7.

Milam: "You still as good as I am?"

Bobo: "Yeah."

Milam: "You still 'had' white women [as girlfriends]?"

Bobo: "Yeah."

That big .45 [handgun] jumped in Milam's hand. The youth turned to catch that big, expanding bullet at his right ear. He dropped.

They barb-wired the gin fan [a device to prepare cotton] to his neck, rolled him into 20 feet of water.

For three hours that morning, there was a fire in Big Milam's back yard: Bobo's crepe soled shoes were hard to burn.

Seventy-two hours later—eight miles downstream—boys were fishing. They saw feet sticking out of the water. Bobo.

William Bradford Huie, "The Shocking Story of Approved Killing in Mississippi," Public Broadcasting System. www.pbs.org/wgbh/amex/till/sfeature/sf_look_confession.html.

resulted a year later in a federal court order desegregating buses throughout the South.

The boycott was the first victory in the civil rights movement, which over the next decade would finally result in blacks gaining some semblance of equal rights and protection against racially motivated violence. But the victories blacks earned were all stained with blood because many southern racists fought them with every weapon they could, including murder.

Upholding Jim Crow with Violence

The racial violence that had long plagued the South had declined during the late 1940s. It flared anew in the 1950s when blacks began breaking down racial barriers that segregationists had held so dear. The first crack in Jim Crow had come in the May 17, 1954, U.S. Supreme Court decision that declared segregated schools illegal. The federal government ordered southern public schools to accept students whatever their race. Although southern communities would manage to postpone integrating their schools for years to come, the court's action left many southern whites worried about the future.

Unease over school integration revitalized the KKK, which had been in decline. In September 1956 members of the Klan conducted an enormous cross-burning ceremony, the largest held since World War II. Imperial Wizard Eldon Lee Edwards told nearly twenty-five hundred people gathered on Stone Mountain in Georgia that the Klan was opposed to equality for blacks. Said Edwards: "We have been accused for over ninety years as cutthroats and those who take the law into their own hands. If the Supreme Court can't maintain our southern way of life, then we are going to do something about it."[74] The intent of his words was unmistakable—the Klan and other racist groups would attack and kill anyone who promoted integration or racial equality.

The violence Edwards recommended had already begun on January 30, 1956, when someone bombed the Montgomery home of the Reverend Martin Luther King Jr., who had led the bus boycott there. Several sticks of dynamite tossed from a passing car damaged King's home but did not hurt anyone. Afterward, King's wife, Coretta, received a telephone call from the bomber. "Yes, I did it. And I'm just sorry I didn't kill all you bastards."[75]

Teenagers protest school desegregation in Montgomery, Alabama, in 1963.

Murder Was No Longer Public

As the attack on King's home made clear, white supremacists believed that murder was an acceptable response to blacks' demands for integration. A leaflet distributed at a February 10, 1956, meeting in Mississippi attended by twelve thousand people openly advocated killing blacks. Stating "LET'S GET ON THE BALL WHITE CITIZENS," the leaflet said that "to abolish the Negro race, proper methods should be used. Among these are guns, bows and arrows, sling shots and knives."[76]

Now, however, racists no longer openly conducted lynchings like those that had once been witnessed by thousands of people. Instead, the members of hate groups like the KKK did their work in secret, going to great trouble to conceal their identities. The

Police and firefighters investigate the 1963 bombing of the Sixteenth Street Baptist Church in Birmingham, Alabama.

reason for this change was a greater willingness on the part of the federal government to protect African Americans. Although there still was no law that specifically made lynching a crime, federal authorities could—and did—prosecute those who violated the civil rights of blacks.

The most anonymous way to kill was with a bomb, which could be tossed from a moving car or planted and detonated by a timer long after the killer had left the area. It became a favored weapon of whites in their battle against civil rights. Birmingham, the scene of many major battles for civil rights, was rocked by so many such attacks that it was nicknamed "Bombingham."

Not only were bombs anonymous; they were also indiscriminate in who they killed or maimed. The deadliest blast occurred on the morning of September 15, 1963, just before Sunday services at the Sixteenth Street Baptist Church. Fifteen sticks of dynamite exploded, blowing apart the church basement and killing four girls who were changing into their choir robes—Denise McNair, Carole Robertson, Addie Mae Collins, and Cynthia Wesley. The bombing horrified the nation, which could not understand how any person could have been vicious enough to attack a church and kill children. Chris McNair later blamed not only the bomber but every white in Birmingham for the death of his eleven-year-old daughter: "I don't think that the average citizen would want it to happen at anybody's church, but I also think that as long as the average citizens were condoning the kind of [racist] government that we had at that time, then I think they were just as guilty as anybody else."[77]

What motivated the bombers was fear. More than anything else, racists feared that blacks would be able to vote, which

In 1955 Rosa Parks (front) was arrested for refusing to give up her seat on a bus for a white man.

would give them enough political power to end segregation. Because of this, civil rights workers, white as well as black, who were trying to accomplish that goal were prime targets for all sorts of attacks. Mississippi became a focal point for the fight to stop blacks from voting, and among the voting activists who were murdered was Herbert Lee.

The killing of Lee followed a familiar pattern in which the murderer justified his crime with an excuse that allowed him to go free but was so flimsy that the message to other activists was clear. Lee, a black farmer, was shot to death in Amite County, Mississippi, on September 25, 1961. He was killed by F.H. Hurst, a state legislator, when they argued over cotton Lee was selling. Historians believe the real reason Lee was shot was that he was helping people register to vote. Robert Moses, a fellow civil rights worker, described Lee's slaying, which occurred while Lee was getting out of his truck:

> [Hurst] pulled out a gun which he had under his shirt and began threatening Lee with it. One of the people that was close by said that Hurst was telling Lee, "I'm not fooling around this time, I really mean business." [When Lee began to get out of his truck] Hurst ran around the front of the cab, took his gun out again, pointed it at Lee and shot him.[78]

Anyone Could Be a Target

Sometimes the perpetrators of such violence made no effort to conceal their real motives. Such was the case with those who murdered Viola Gregg Liuzzo, whose death illustrated that just about anybody could be a target of racist violence. On the night of March 25, 1965, Liuzzo, a white civil rights worker from Detroit, was giving people rides back to Selma from Montgomery after they had marched there in a protest against restrictions on voting rights. Liuzzo was accompanied by LeRoy Moton, a black civil rights activist. After dropping off people in Selma, Liuzzo was driving back to Montgomery when a car carrying four Klansmen drew alongside the vehicle, and the Klansmen started firing guns at her car. Moton later explained what happened: "I reached for the radio and that's when I felt this glass and everything hit me in the face, and the car was goin' off the road. Mrs. Liuzzo,

Officials excavate the site where the bodies of James Chaney, Michael Schwerner, and Andrew Goodman were hidden.

last thing she said was, 'I was just thinkin' of this song, "Before I'll be a slave, I'll be buried in my grave."' By the time she got 'grave' out, that's when she was shot."[79]

Moton was thrown from the vehicle when it crashed. His only injuries were cuts from glass, but he was bleeding so much that when accomplices of the assailants got out of a car to see if he and Liuzzo were alive, they concluded he was dead. The blood, Moton believes, saved his life.

Although Liuzzo's murder was carried out brazenly, the typical scenario was for the targeted person to die under mysterious circumstances—or simply to disappear. This was the case in the most infamous murder of civil rights workers. This happened in 1964 during "Freedom Summer," when over eight hundred college students went to Mississippi to help register black voters. On June 21, civil rights workers Andrew Goodman, Michael Schwerner, and James Chaney disappeared while investigating the burning of a church that had been part of the voter registration effort. Their bodies were found after a long search on August 4; Goodman and Schwerner had been shot while Chaney, the only black, had been beaten and then shot.

Subsequent investigations revealed that a group of KKK members had followed their car and then forced them off the road in a remote area and murdered them. The two Klansmen who killed them were Alton Wayne Roberts and James Jordan. Roberts shot Goodman and Schwerner, but both men shot Chaney. According to court testimony at his trial years later, Jordan told Roberts, "Well, you didn't leave me nothing but a nigger, but at least I killed me a nigger."[80]

Dave Dennis, a field director for the Council of Federated Organizations, which was coordinating the registration drive, said he felt personally responsible for the deaths of the three men. Dennis had assigned them to investigate the fire and lent them the car they were in. Dennis believes they might have been targeted because they were in his car: "At the time that they [KKK members] stopped the car, they thought that I was in that car. You can't help but blame yourself."[81] Dennis believed that he was just one of many civil rights workers targeted by the KKK.

Assassinating the Leaders

Another of those targeted was an NAACP leader named Medgar Evers, who on June 12, 1963, was shot as he got out of his car in the driveway of his home in Jackson, Mississippi. Evers was the statewide head of the NAACP and had been successful in working to end segregation in the Jackson area.

Evers's death was supposed to frighten other blacks away from pursuing that same goal, but that did not happen. The night Evers was killed, his wife, Myrlie, spoke to about five hundred people in a meeting at the Pearl Street Church. Evers declared that she was determined to finish the work her husband had started: "I am left with the strong determination to try to take up where he left off. I hope that by his death [other people] will be able to draw some of his strength, some of his courage and some of his determination to finish this fight. Nothing can bring Medgar back, but the cause can live on."[82]

Less than three years later, on January 10, 1966, southerners killed another black Mississippi civil rights leader—Vernon Dahmer. At

Myrlie Evers Watched
Her Husband Die

◼

Shortly before 1:00 A.M. on June 12, 1963, Medgar Evers was shot to death at his Jackson, Mississippi, home. Evers headed the National Association for the Advancement of Colored People in Mississippi. He was shot after he got out of his car. His wife, Myrlie, describes the murder:

> Late that night, he came home. The children were still up, I was [lying] across the bed, and we heard the motor of the car coming in and pulling into the driveway. We heard him get out of the car and the car door slam, and in that same instant, we heard the loud gunfire. The children fell to the floor, as he had taught them to do. I made a run for the front door, turned on the light, and there he was. The bullet had pushed him forward, as I understand, and the strong man that he was, he had his keys in his hand and had pulled his body around the rest of the way, to the door. There he lay. I screamed, and people came out. Our next door neighbor fired a gun, as he said, to try to frighten anyone away, and I knew that that was it.

Henry Hampton and Steve Fayer, *Voices of Freedom: An Oral History of the Civil Rights Movement from the 1950s through the 1980s.* New York: Bantam, 1990, p. 154.

Myrlie Evers speaks at an anti-segregation rally in Washington D.C. in 1963.

2:00 A.M., a band of KKK members came to his house in Kelley Settlement and set it on fire. When the blaze woke up the fifty-eight-year-old NAACP leader, he reached for his shotgun and told his wife to flee to safety: "Jewell! Get the children out while I hold them off." They made it out alive, but Dahmer did not survive. Badly burned, he died fourteen hours later in the hospital. "They finally got me,"[83] he said just before he died.

So determined were the segregationists to defeat those working for integration that even the most prominent in the civil rights movement were targeted. The most famous civil rights leader murdered was the Reverend Martin Luther King Jr. King was in Memphis, Tennessee, to lead a protest designed to call attention to the plight of black city workers who were striking for better pay. King was shot to death on April 4, 1968, while standing on the balcony of his hotel room.

King's death shocked the nation and ignited riots in several major American cities. Eight hundred people came to King's funeral, where they heard the fallen leader eulogized. Perhaps the truest words spoken that day came in a remark by the Reverend Martin Luther King Sr., the slain civil rights leader's father. Said King: "It was the *hate* in this land that took my son away from me."[84]

The Failure of Hatred

The violence that racial hatred spawned, however, failed to deter southern blacks in their quest for equality with whites. One who typified the determination of blacks to exercise their rights as American citizens was the Reverend Fred Shuttlesworth, a native of Birmingham, Alabama. Shuttlesworth was beaten many times, once with chains for trying to register his children in an all-white public school. He was also knocked unconscious during a civil rights protest in 1963 in Birmingham when a stream of water from a fire hose slammed him into a building. Eugene "Bull" Connor, the city's commissioner of public safety, had ordered fire-fighters to use the high-pressure hoses to break up the protest. When Connor learned that Shuttlesworth had been taken to a hospital in an ambulance, he said, "I wish it had been a hearse."[85] Shuttlesworth later recalled: "I had the drive to get things done and fear just didn't bother me."[86]

Chapter Six

Justice Delayed: Prosecuting Lynchers Decades Later

The July 27, 1946, edition of the *New York Times* newspaper carried a disturbing story from Monroe, Georgia. Its first paragraph read: "Two young Negroes, one a veteran just returned from [World War II], and their wives were lined up [on July 25] near a secluded road and shot dead by an unmasked band of twenty white men."[87] The victims were Roger and Dorothy Malcom and George and Mae Murray Dorsey. The newspaper said it was the year's first lynching as well as first multiple lynching since October 1942, when a Mississippi mob had hung two fourteen-year-old black youths.

On July 26, 2005, many newspapers carried another story datelined Monroe. It explained how African Americans played the parts of the victims as well as the whites who killed them in a reenactment of the nation's last mass lynching. The macabre event was staged on the fifty-ninth anniversary of the slayings to protest the fact that no one had ever been charged with

In 2005, reenactors portrayed the 1946 lynching of Roger and Dorothy Malcom and George and Mae Dorsey in an effort to reopen an investigation of their deaths.

killing the two couples. The Reverend Jesse Jackson and other civil rights leaders demanded an investigation into their deaths even though five decades had passed. "The blood of the lynched cries out," said Jackson.[88] No one was ever charged even though the original Federal Bureau of Investigation (FBI) report on the quadruple lynching listed the names of fifty-five suspects. The report claimed the mob wanted to punish Roger Malcom for injuring a white man in a fight eleven days earlier; the other blacks were killed simply because they were with him.

The failure by authorities to prosecute suspects was typical of the lack of justice in the era of lynchings that began after the Civil War. The reason was that most officials responsible for enforcing the law condoned such violent acts because they shared the racist attitudes of the perpetrators. Even on the rare occasions when officials prosecuted suspects, all-white juries routinely found them innocent no matter how strong the evidence against them.

This situation changed dramatically in the last three decades of the twentieth century. In the wake of court decisions requiring that blacks be allowed to serve on juries, lynchers no longer could expect their crimes to be overlooked. Blacks also used their voting power to elect officials such as Bill Baxley, who in 1970 became Alabama's attorney general. Baxley and other like-minded officials began a crusade that continues into the twenty-first century to punish perpetrators of decades-old crimes.

A Birthday Present for Denise

Unlike his predecessors who had allowed the KKK to operate freely, Baxley was the Klan's enemy. "What they do is so distasteful to everything America stands for, or should stand for, I just hate 'em,"[89] he once said. Baxley harnessed that hatred to help

Friends and family mourn the deaths of Dorothy Malcom and George Dorsey at their funeral.

him expose the Klan's involvement in the deadliest civil rights era lynching—the Sixteenth Street Baptist Church bombing on September 15, 1963, that killed four girls.

When Baxley became attorney general, he requested the original FBI files on the Birmingham bombing. Getting these records was no easy matter. There were those in the agency who did not want the public to learn of its past failure to prosecute suspects, even though it had the power to do so under laws protecting the civil rights of the victims.

Baxley was stunned by what he learned when he finally obtained the files. The FBI had closed its investigation in 1968 without taking any action, even though a 1965 memorandum to FBI director J. Edgar Hoover concluded that four Klansmen— Robert E. Chambliss, Bobby Frank Cherry, Herman Frank Cash, and Thomas E. Blanton—had conducted the bombing. Chambliss, who was nicknamed "Dynamite Bob," was suspected in other bombings. He had been tried for murder in the bombing on state

Attendants remove the body of a victim of the Sixteenth Street Church bombing in 1963.

charges but was found innocent on October, 8, 1963, by a white jury. Baxley also dicovered that the FBI had withheld evidence from the prosecution that could have linked Chambliss to the bombing. The order to do that had come from Hoover, who was unsympathetic to the civil rights movement and feared a conviction would strengthen it.

The new information allowed Baxley to reopen the investigation into the bombing and charge Chambliss with murder under federal laws. His star witness in the 1977 trial was Chambliss's niece, Elizabeth Cobbs, who testified that after the bombing she heard her uncle say, "It wasn't meant to hurt anybody. It didn't go off when it was supposed to."[90]

In his passionate closing argument, Baxley told the jury their verdict would be historically important. Said Baxley: "You've got a chance to do something. Let the world know that this is not the way the people of Alabama felt then or feel now. It's not going to bring those little girls back, but it will show the world that this murder case has been solved by the people of Alabama. Give Denise a birthday present."[91]

On November 18, a jury convicted Chambliss. He was sentenced to life in prison, where he died in 1985. The guilty verdict came on the birthday of bomb victim Denise McNair, who would have been twenty-six years old. Justice, however, had only been partially fulfilled, because the three other suspects remained free.

He Was Not Watching Wrestling

Alabama officials were unable to gather enough evidence to charge the other three suspects until 1996, when, at the urging of new leaders, the FBI decided to join the investigation. The FBI helped Alabama build a case against Cherry and Blanton, but Cash had died in 1994. The effort to bring the guilty to justice was also strengthened by evidence uncovered by Jerry Mitchell, a reporter for the *Clarion-Ledger* newspaper in Jackson, Mississippi, who had begun his own investigation of the case.

When Mitchell interviewed Cherry in 1999, Cherry repeated his claim that he had been home watching wrestling on television when the bomb exploded. Mitchell did some detective work that officials had failed to do: He checked old TV schedules and discovered that there had been no televised wrestling that day. Mitchell's discovery

Breaking a Murderer's Alibi

◼

Because Jerry Mitchell was a good reporter, Bobby Frank Cherry was convicted of killing four young girls in the Sixteenth Street Baptist Church bombing. A story Mitchell wrote in 1999 proved Cherry lied when he claimed he could not have participated in the September 15, 1963, bombing because he was home watching wrestling on television. When Mitchell checked the television schedule for that day, he discovered there had been no wrestling. His story helped reopen the investigation into Cherry's part in the bombing. In an interview on the Public Broadcasting System on April 18, 2002, Mitchell explained how he caught Cherry in the lie when he interviewed him:

> [Cherry] said, "Well, I didn't have anything to do with that bombing. I left [work and] had to go home and watch wrestling." I got back here to the newspaper and [told Susan Garcia], "You know, Susan, check with the Birmingham News and just see what was on TV that night." The next morning when I got in, I had an electronic message from Susan. Not only was there not wrestling on [television] that night, there wasn't wrestling on for years. [For] three and a half decades his alibi had basically gone unchallenged, and now, lo and behold his alibi doesn't stand up.

Bob Cherry was convicted of the Sixteenth Street Church bombing in 2001.

Quoted in Jerry Mitchell, "Online NewsHour: Pursuing the Past," Public Broadcasting System, April 18, 2002. www.pbs.org/newshour/media/clarion/mitchell.html.

proved that Cherry had faked his alibi and gave new life to the effort to solve the case. Both Cherry and Blanton were charged with murder in 2000, convicted in 2001, and sentenced to life in prison. Blanton was found guilty on May 1. The conviction pleased Alpha Robertson, the eighty-two-year-old mother of bombing victim Carole Robertson: "I'm very happy that justice came down today. I didn't know if it would come in my lifetime."[92]

The convictions might not have been possible without Michell's crack investigative reporting. But Cherry and Blanton were not the first perpetrators of racial violence that Mitchell helped bring to justice. The first murderer Mitchell helped convict was the man who killed Medgar Evers.

Justice for Medgar Evers

After Evers was shot to death on June 12, 1963, a suspect—Byron De La Beckwith—had been quickly arrested. Some observers had expected a conviction because his fingerprints had been found on the murder weapon, a deer rifle the killer had left near the murder scene. But in two separate trials in 1964, all-white juries allowed De La Beckwith to go free by failing to find him guilty.

In 1989, Mitchell discovered documents which showed that state officials had secretly and illegally helped lawyers defending De La Beckwith by withholding key evidence detectives had gathered. When Myrlie Evers read Mitchell's story, she requested a new investigation into her husband's death.

Hinds County district attorney Bobby DeLaughter reopened the case even though he knew it would be difficult to prosecute such an old case successfully. Said DeLaughter: "At the very beginning we didn't have anything. The [district attorney's] file was nowhere to be found. We did not have the benefit of a trial transcript to know who the witnesses were. None of the evidence had been retained by the court."[93]

But DeLaughter's office dug up new facts in the case, including testimony from witnesses who had heard De La Beckwith boast about killing Evers. De La Beckwith was arrested on December 17, 1990, and on February 5, 1994, a jury found him guilty—more than three decades after he had murdered Evers.

Justice was done in the Evers slaying, even though officials years earlier had helped De La Beckwith escape punishment. But

In 1994 Byron De La Beckwith (right) was found guilty of the 1963 murder of Medgar Evers.

in the 1964 murders of civil rights workers Andrew Goodman, Michael Schwerner, and James Chaney, officials had to revisit a case that had seemingly been solved many years earlier to gain true justice.

Justice at Long Last

The story of the slaying of Goodman, Schwerner, and Chaney began on June 21, 1964, in Neshoba County, Mississippi. On that day they were investigating a fire that had destroyed Mount Zion Methodist Church in Longdale, which had been slated to host voter registration activities. The three were driving back to Meridian, Mississippi, when Neshoba County deputy sheriff Cecil Price pulled them over and took them to the jail in nearby Philadelphia, supposedly on suspicion of having been involved in the fire.

Price, a member of the KKK, alerted local Klan leaders that he had arrested the civil rights workers. The conspirators decided to kill them as a warning to others who were trying to help blacks register to vote. Price released the men about 8:00 P.M., telling them to leave town. But when they left, some twenty KKK members chased them down, took them to a remote area, and shot them.

FBI agents learned the names of the men involved from informants. U.S. Justice Department officials decided to file federal charges against them because they feared that state courts and juries would not convict them. The government, because there was no federal statute at the time under which they could be charged with murder, charged eighteen men with conspiring to deprive the victims of their civil rights. A jury on October 20, 1967, convicted seven defendants, including Price. They were sentenced to serve from three to ten years in prison. The *New York Times* hailed the verdict as proof of the South's "slow, still faltering but inexorable conversion to the concept that a single standard of justice must cover whites and Negroes alike."[94]

Many people, however, believed the short prison sentences were not true justice in the brutal slayings. One of them was Mitchell. While looking into a different incident of racial violence—the 1966 slaying of black civil rights leader Vernon Dahmer—he came across evidence a Klansman named Edgar Ray Killen had ordered the killing of the three men. Mitchell continued investigating Killen and in 2004 wrote a story that included claims by other Klansmen that Killen had directed the murders.

Based on Mitchell's new findings, Mississippi officials reopened the case and on January 6, 2005, charged Killen with three counts of murder. The indictment was especially meaningful to Lawrence Guyot, a civil rights worker who knew the three victims and had almost gone with them to investigate the fire: "I prayed to live until this day. We fought for this. We dreamed of this. And now it is reality. It's a statement that political assassinations are not acceptable in the state of Mississippi. Never again."[95]

On June 21, 2005, the forty-first anniversary of the slayings, a jury found Killen guilty of three counts of manslaughter. The seventy-five-year-old was sentenced to three twenty-year terms in prison. Killen's conviction was the twenty-second that federal and state authorities have won since 1989 in their continuing campaign to seek justice in the brutal murders and lynchings of blacks in the past.

One of those victories came on August 21, 1998, when Sam Bowers was found guilty of murdering Dahmer. The civil rights activist died on January 10, 1966, when his Hattiesburg, Mississippi, home was set on fire. The conviction came after four previous trials in which white juries had failed to convict Bowers. When Bowers was finally found guilty, Ellie Dahmer, the victim's widow, saw it as a positive sign of racial change in Mississippi: "We have a generation who can look at the facts and see things are wrong and make a conviction."[96]

The Pursuit of Justice Continues

Despite the many successes southerners have scored in reclaiming justice from past misdeeds, many people fear that time is running out on bringing other murderers to trial. The reason is that suspects in such cases and the witnesses who can provide the testimony needed to convict them are growing older. Every year, there are fewer people who are able to tell their stories and help bring closure to the victims' families.

Heidi Beirich, a spokesperson for the Southern Poverty Law Center in Montgomery, Alabama, said in September 2005 that "we want these cases solved before it's too late."[97] That was the reason why U.S. senators Jim Talent, a Missouri Republican, and Christopher Dodd, a Connecticut Democrat, proposed a bill in May 2005 to create a unit in the Justice Department's Civil Rights Division whose job would be to investigate and prosecute old cases of murder and violence against blacks. The Senate rejected the measure in 2005, but the two senators vowed they would continue to try to pass the bill. Said Dodd of the measure: "It cannot bring back and make whole those who suffered and died by a racist's criminal hand. But it can at least reaffirm our nation's commitment to seek the truth and make equal justice a reality."[98]

Reopening the Till Case

The urgency to act quickly so justice can be done was evident in the new investigation into the death of Emmett Till, one of the twentieth century's most famous lynching victims. The fourteen-year-old Chicago boy was brutally killed on August 28, 1955, in Money, Mississippi, because he had playfully whistled at a white female store clerk. Although two white men, Roy Bryant and J.W. Milam, were charged with his murder, an all-white jury acquitted them despite strong evidence of their guilt. Two months after the

An Important Decision

—■—

On October 18, 1967, U.S. attorney John Doar delivered his closing argument in the conspiracy trial of eighteen men charged with murdering civil rights workers Michael Schwerner, Andrew Goodman, and James Chaney. Doar told jurors their decision was important because it would show the world how Mississippi felt about the murders:

> Members of the Jury, this is an important case. It is important to the government. It's important to the defendants, but most important, it's important to the State of Mississippi. What I say, what the other lawyers say here today, what the Court says about the law will soon be forgotten, but what you twelve people do here today will long be remembered. . . . If you find that these men or that each of them is not guilty of this conspiracy it would be as true to say that there was no night time release from jail by [deputy sheriff] Cecil Price, there were no White Knights, there are no young men dead, there was no murder. If you find that these men are not guilty you will declare the law of Neshoba County to be the law of the State of Mississippi.

On October 20, jurors convicted seven defendants, including Price.

University of Missouri-Kansas City School of Law, "Closing Argument by Mr. Doar." www.law.umkc.edu/faculty/projects/ftrials/price&bowers/doarclose.html.

trial, author William Bradford Huie wrote a story for *Look* magazine in which Milam even admitted that he had killed Till. In the interview with Huie, Milam explained how he told Till he was going to die before he shot him: "I just looked at him and I said, 'Boy, you ain't never going to see the sun come up again.'"[99]

The two men acknowledged they had killed Till, but they could not be tried again for his murder. Over the years, however, family and friends of Till held out hope that the case would one day be reopened, because they suspected other people had participated in the lynching. If they could be identified, they could still be tried for Till's murder.

The U.S. Justice Department on May 10, 2004, finally gave in to those demands and reopened the case to determine if anyone else helped kill Till. On May 31, 2005 Till's body was exhumed from its grave in the suburban Chicago cemetery where he was buried. The Cook County medical examiner's office in Chicago conducted an autopsy on his body and sent the results to the FBI. It was hoped the new data could yield clues to new suspects because no autopsy had been done when he died. Till's body was reburied on June 4.

FBI officials completed their investigation in December 2005, but the federal government has yet to decide if there is enough evidence to link anyone else to the crime or to convict them of a crime that is now over a half century old. But despite the uncertainty over whether the effort would yield any solid results, many people believed it was proper to try to find out if there were other suspects. In an editorial in its November 28, 2005, edition, the *Commercial Appeal* of Memphis, Tennessee, explained why the attempt was necessary: "The criminal justice system has not finished its job until the matter is fully explored. Neither the pas-

J.W. Milam and his wife calmly react after Milam was acquitted of Emmett Till's murder in 1955.

FBI officials exhume the body of Emmett Till in 2005 for a new investigation into his murder.

sage of time nor the complexities of the case should deter the effort to see justice done for Emmett Till."[100]

Respect for Lynching Victims

The interest in seeking justice for violence against blacks is an indication of the South's new racial attitudes. The difference from the past to the present can be seen in the remarks of two judges who, decades apart, sentenced suspects for killing Chaney, Goodman, and Schwerner. Judge Harold Cox defended what many people considered to be lenient sentences he gave to defendants on December 29, 1967, by claiming, "They killed one nigger, one Jew, and a white man—I gave them all what I thought they deserved." When Judge Marcus Gordon on June 23, 2005, sentenced Killen to three twenty-year terms for his role in the same deaths, he noted, "I have taken into consideration that there are three lives in this case and that the three lives should be absolutely respected."[101]

The new respect for the lives of all people, not just whites, is the key difference in race relations in the South today.

The Legacy of Lynching

For nearly a century following the Civil War, southern whites lynched thousands of blacks in their attempt to continue dominating them. Throughout this period, the U.S. Senate failed to stop this racial violence despite pleas from seven presidents. It also rejected three anti-lynching bills the House of Representatives passed. On June 13, 2005, the nation's highest legislative body finally acted. In a voice vote, the Senate approved a resolution that apologized to the descendants of lynching victims for past failures to protect African Americans. The resolution was introduced by Senators Mary Landrieu, a Louisiana Democrat, and George Allen, a Virginia Republican. On the day the Senate voted, Landrieu commented:

> That was wrong to not stand in the way of the mob. We [senators] lacked courage then. We perhaps don't have all the courage we need today to do everything that we should do. But I know that we can apologize today. We can be sincere in our apology to the families, to their loved ones, and perhaps now we can set some of these victims and their families free [from the past] and most of all set our country free to be better than it is today.[102]

Two hundred descendants and family friends of lynching victims witnessed the historic vote. One was Doria Dee Johnson, the great-great-granddaughter of Anthony Crawford, who on October 21, 1916, was lynched by a mob in Abbeville, South Carolina. The perpetrators had hung Crawford from a tree limb and then fired two hundred bullets into his swaying body. His only crime had been to argue with a store owner he thought was trying to cheat him on the sale of cotton. No one was ever charged with killing him.

Johnson said she was happy that the senators passed the resolution. But she also acknowledged that the passage of so much time between the lynching and the apology had robbed her ancestor of true justice: "It's really all the Senate can do now, is apologize."[103] Like many other people, Johnson knew that the apology could do little to heal the wounds caused by so many lynchings.

James Cameron (seated), who was the oldest living person to survive an attempted lynching, speaks to members of the U.S. Senate at a press conference in 2005.

Lynching's Bitter Legacy

Although the desire to maintain white supremacy motivated most of the violence against blacks, another powerful factor underlying many brutal incidents was simply greed. Some whites used the power they had over blacks to steal land, money, and other wealth. In a series of stories in 2001, the Associated Press wire service documented how southern whites over a period of 150 years had stolen money, small businesses, and more than twenty-four thousand acres of farm and timberland from over four hundred blacks.

Johnson believes her ancestor was lynched because whites wanted his farm. After he was murdered, local officials seized and sold most of his possessions, including already-harvested cotton worth $5,438. The officials gave each of his children just $200 and kept the rest of the money. Crawford's family still owned his farm, which was valued at $20,000, but soon lost it because they could not repay a $2,000 bank loan for which the land was collateral. The farm was then sold at auction to a white bidder for $504. Johnson said the lynching destroyed her family by taking away their home and the farm on which they made their living: "There's land taken away and there's murder. But the biggest crime was that our family was split up by this. My family got scattered into the night."[104] The lives of thousands of other blacks were also ruined in this way.

Another legacy is that even though such racial violence has become rare, the fear of it still exists. In April 2004, when the body of fifty-five-year-old Roy Veal was found hanging from a tree in rural Woodville, Mississippi, rumors spread that he had been lynched by whites in a land dispute. But Wilkinson County sheriff Reginald Jackson, the county's first black sheriff, reported that Veal's death was a suicide. Jackson said he understood why some people believed a lynching could have happened: "Wilkinson County and the state of Mississippi have struggled hundreds of years with race relations. We have endured many lynchings, beatings, and much discrimination. Although things are not what they should be, we are indeed better than we used to be."[105]

Such lynching fears are not completely unfounded, because sporadic violence against blacks continues even today. The KKK remains active in southern states along with neo-Nazi organiza-

Officials escort John William King to court, where he was tried and convicted of dragging a black man to death behind his truck in 1998.

tions dedicated to white supremacy. In 1999 Shawn Allen Berry, John William King, and Lawrence Russel Brewer were convicted of murdering James Byrd Jr. on June 7, 1998, in Jasper, Texas. The three tied Byrd to a pickup truck with a chain and dragged him about three miles. They admitted they did this because they hated blacks. On the day King was convicted, Byrd's sister, Stella Brumley, said it was important to punish him: "You have to send a strong message or else we'll be back to the [lynching days of the] 1800s."[106] King was a KKK member.

A Different Lynching Legacy

James Cameron is one of many people who believe the best way to prevent such racial violence is to educate the public about past injustices. Cameron has a unique perspective on the subject because on August 6, 1930, he survived an attempted lynching in Marion, Indiana. Cameron was with two friends when they decided to rob a white man. Although Cameron had left his companions before they robbed and killed the man, he was also arrested. A mob then seized the blacks from jail and took them to the city's courthouse square for a lynching.

After hanging his two friends, whites put a noose around Cameron's neck. At the news conference following passage of the Senate apology more than six decades later, the ninety-one-year-old Cameron explained what happened: "I was saved by a miracle. They were going to lynch me between my two buddies, they were hollering for my blood when a voice [in a crowd of fifteen thousand people] said, 'Take this boy back.'"[107] Cameron never learned who spoke those words, but the crowd miraculously heeded the words and returned him to the safety of the jail.

After serving a twenty-one-year prison sentence in connection with the fatal robbery, Cameron dedicated his life to fighting for civil rights. One way he did that was to open America's Black Holocaust Museum in Milwaukee, Wisconsin, to document lynching and other racial injustice. Cameron said the museum's goal is a simple one: "The living legacy [of lynching] is that we never forget. Our mission here is to educate the general public of the violent injustices suffered by the people of African American heritage and to provide visitors with an opportunity to rethink their assumptions about race and racism."[108]

Notes

Introduction:
The Tools of Racial Terrorism

1. Quoted in Mark Twain, "The United States of Lyncherdom," Etext Center at the University of Virginia Library. www.etext.lib.virginia.edu/railton/enam482e/lyncherdom.html.

2. Quoted in Avis Thomas-Lester, "A Landscape Scarred by Lynchings: Va. Lives with Legacy of Terror and Grief," *Washington Post*, July 24, 2005, LZ p. 1.

3. Quoted in Philip Dray, *At the Hands of Persons Unknown: The Lynching of Black America*. New York: Random House, 2002, p. xi.

Chapter 1: The Brutality of Lynching and Murder

4. Quoted in The History of Jim Crow, "Ell Persons." www.jimcrowhistory. org/scripts/jimcrow/map.cgi?city= memphis&state=tennessee.

5. Quoted in Michael J. Pfeifer, *Rough Justice: Lynching and American Society, 1874–1947*. Urbana: University of Illinois Press, 2004, p. 6.

6. Quoted in James Elbert Cutler, *Lynch-Law: An Investigation into the History of Lynching in the United States*. New York: Longmans, Green, 1905, p. 196.

7. Cutler, *Lynch-Law*, p. 168.

8. David Garland, "Penal Excess and Surplus Meaning: Public Torture Lynchings in Twentieth-Century America," *Law & Society Review*, December 2005, p. 793.

9. Quoted in Dray, *At the Hands of Persons Unknown*, p. 78.

10. Quoted in Ralph Ginzburg, *100 Years of Lynchings*. Baltimore: Black Classic, 1988, p. 221.

11. Quoted in Stewart E. Tolnay and E.M. Beck, *A Festival of Violence: An Analysis of Southern Lynchings, 1882–1930*. Chicago: University of Illinois Press, 1995, p. 26.

12. Quoted in Garland, "Penal Excess and Surplus Meaning," p. 796.

13. Quoted in Dray, *At the Hands of Persons Unknown*, p. 218.

14. Quoted in James Allen, Hilton Als, John Lewis, and Leon F. Litwack, *Without Sanctuary: Lynching Photography in America*. Santa Fe, NM: Twin Palms, 2000, p. 15.

15. Quoted in Dray, *At the Hands of Persons Unknown*, p. 178.

16. Quoted in Richard Wormser, "Red Summer (1919)," The Rise and Fall of Jim Crow. www.pbs.org/wnet/jimcrow/stories_events_red.html.

17. Walter White, *A Man Called White*. New York: Arno, 1969, p. 234.

18. Quoted in Dray, *At the Hands of Persons Unknown*, p. 234.

Chapter 2:
Maintaining Social and Racial Order Through Violence

19. Quoted in The History of Jim Crow, "Eyewitness to Jim Crow: Joseph Holloway Remembers." www.jim crowhistory.org/resources/narratives/ Joe_Holloway.html.
20. Quoted in The History of Jim Crow, "Eyewitness to Jim Crow."
21. Walter White, *Rope and Faggot: A Biography of Judge Lynch*. New York: Arno and the *New York Times*, 1969, p. 95.
22. Quoted in Spartacus Educational, "Black Codes." www.spartacus.school net.co.uk/USASblackcodes.html.
23. Quoted in Eric Foner, *Reconstruction: America's Unfinished Revolution*. New York: Harper and Row, 1988, p. 120.
24. Quoted in Dray, *At the Hands of Persons Unknown*, p. 98.
25. Quoted in Dorothy Sterling, ed., *The Trouble They Seen: Black People Tell the Story of Reconstruction*. Garden City, NY: Doubleday, 1976, p. 113.
26. Quoted in Dray, *At the Hands of Persons Unknown*, p. 43.
27. Quoted in Anne P. Rice, ed., *Witnessing Lynching: American Writers Respond*. New Brunswick, NJ: Rutgers University Press, 2003, p. 73.
28. Quoted in Foner, *Reconstruction*, p. 602.
29. Quoted in Ginzburg, *100 Years of Lynchings*, p. 168.
30. Quoted in Dolores Barclay, Todd

Lewan, and Allen G. Breed, "Investigation: Black Landowners Targeted," *Clarion-Ledger Mississipi News*, December 3, 2001, p. 1.
31. Quoted in Allen, Als, Lewis, and Litwack, *Without Sanctuary*, p. 27.
32. Quoted in Dray, *At the Hands of Persons Unknown*, p. 223.
33. Quoted in "Freedom Never Dies: The Legacy of Harry T. Moore," Public Broadcasting System. www.pbs.org/harrymoore.
34. Quoted in Faulkner Fox, "Justice in Jasper," *Texas Observer*, September 17, 1999, p. 1.

Chapter 3: The Face of Hatred:
The Perpetrators of Violence

35. Quoted in Ginzburg, *100 Years of Lynchings*, p. 25.
36. Quoted in Allen, Als, Lewis, and Litwack, *Without Sanctuary*, p. 11.
37. Quoted in Dray, *At the Hands of Persons Unknown*, p. 41.
38. Quoted in Brian Steel Wills, *A Battle from the Start: The Life of Nathan Bedford Forrest*. New York: HarperCollins, 1992, p. 345.
39. Quoted in Dray, *At the Hands of Persons Unknown*, p. 45.
40. Quoted in Wills, *A Battle from the Start*, p. 368.
41. Robert A. Gibson, "The Negro Holocaust: Lynching and Race Riots in the United States, 1880–1950," Yale-New Haven Teachers Institute. www.yale.edu/ynhti/curriculum/ units/1979/2/79.02.04.x.html.
42. Quoted in Allen, Als, Lewis, and Litwack, *Without Sanctuary*, p. 29.

43. Quoted in Rice, *Witnessing Lynching*, p. 17.

44. Quoted in Allen, Als, Lewis, and Litwack, *Without Sanctuary*, p. 20.

45. White, *Rope and Faggot*, p. 7.

46. Quoted in Dr. David Pilgrim, "The Brute Caricature," Ferris State University Jim Crow Museum of Racist Memorabilia. www.ferris.edu/htmls/news/jimcrow/brute.

47. Quoted in Allen, Als, Lewis, and Litwack, *Without Sanctuary*, p. 24.

48. Quoted in Ginzburg, *100 Years of Lynchings*, p. 159.

49. Quoted in Garland, "Penal Excess and Surplus Meaning," p. 796.

50. Quoted in Rice, *Witnessing Lynching*, p. 255.

51. Quoted in Allen, Als, Lewis, and Litwack, *Without Sanctuary*, p. 13.

52. Quoted in Ginzburg, *100 Years of Lynchings*, p. 29.

53. Quoted in White, *Rope and Faggot*, p. 27.

54. Quoted in Allen, Als, Lewis, and Litwack, *Without Sanctuary*, p. 12.

Chapter 4:
The Effort to End Lynching

55. Quoted in National Association for the Advancement of Colored People, *Thirty Years of Lynching in the United States, 1889–1918.* New York: Arno, 1969, p. 5.

56. Quoted in American Radio Works, "Behind the Veil: Remembering Jim Crow" Transcript, NEH Projects. www.neh.gov/projects/transcripts/behindtheveiltranscript.html.

57. Quoted in American Radio Works, "Behind the Veil."

58. Quoted in Gibson, "The Negro Holocaust."

59. Ida B. Wells, *Crusade for Justice: The Autobiography of Ida B. Wells.* Chicago: University of Chicago Press, 1992, p. 52.

60. Wells, *Crusade for Justice*, p. 62.

61. Quoted in Dray, *At the Hands of Persons Unknown*, p. 171.

62. Quoted in Rice, *Witnessing Lynching*, p. 260.

63. Quoted in Jacquelyn Dowd Hall, *Revolt Against Chivalry: Jessie Daniel Ames and the Women's Campaign Against Lynching.* New York: Columbia University Press, 1979, p. 164.

64. Quoted in Richard Wormser, "Jessie Daniel Ames," The Rise and Fall of Jim Crow. www.pbs.org/wnet/jimcrow/stories_people_ames.html.

65. Quoted in Cutler, *Lynch-Law*, p. 256.

66. Quoted in Documenting the American South, "Defense of the Negro Race—Charges Answered. Speech of Hon. George H. White, of North Carolina, in the House of Representatives, January 29, 1901." http://docsouth.unc.edu/nc/whitegh/whitegh.html.

67. Quoted in Dray, *At the Hands of Persons Unknown*, p. 356.

68. Quoted in Dray, *At the Hands of Persons Unknown*, p. 270.

69. Quoted in Dray, *At the Hands of Persons Unknown*, p. 272.

Chapter 5: Violence During the Civil Rights Era

70. Quoted in Ginzburg, *100 Years of Lynchings*, p. 240.

71. Quoted in Patsy Sims, *The Klan.* Lexington: University Press of Kentucky, 1996, p. 135.

72. Quoted in Douglas Brinkley, *Rosa Parks.* New York: Penguin, 2000, p. 101.

73. Rosa Parks and Gregory J. Reed, *Quiet Strength: The Faith, the Hope, and the Heart of a Woman Who Changed a Nation.* Grand Rapids, MI: Zondervan, 1994, p. 26.

74. Quoted in Wyn Craig Wade, *The Fiery Cross: The Klu Klux Klan in America.* New York: Simon & Schuster, 1987, p. 305.

75. Quoted in Lerone Bennett Jr., *What Manner of Man: A Biography of Martin Luther King, Jr.* Chicago: Johnson, 1976, p. 70.

76. Quoted in Thomas R. Brooks, *Walls Come Tumbling Down: A History of the Civil Rights Movement, 1940–1970.* Englewood Cliffs, NJ: Prentice Hall, 1974, p. 116.

77. Quoted in Howell Raines, *My Soul Is Rested: The Story of the Civil Rights Movement in the Deep South.* New York: Penguin, 1983, p. 185.

78. Quoted in Clayborne Carson, D. Clar, David J. Garrow, Gerald Gill, and Vincent Harding, gen. eds., *The Eyes on the Prize Civil Rights Reader: Documents, Speeches, and Firsthand Accounts from the Black Freedom Struggle, 1954–1990.* New York: Viking, 1991, p. 356.

79. Quoted in Henry Hampton and Steve Fayer, *Voices of Freedom: An Oral History of the Civil Rights Movement from the 1950s through the 1980s.* New York: Bantam, 1990, p. 268.

80. Quoted in Dray, *At the Hands of Persons Unknown*, p. 448.

81. Quoted in Raines, *My Soul Is Rested*, p. 276.

82. Quoted in Dray, *At the Hands of Persons Unknown*, p. xi.

83. Quoted in Paul Hendrickson, *From the Fires of Hate, an Ember of Hope,"* *Washington Post*, July 22, 1998, p. 1A.

84. Quoted in Marshall Frady, *Martin Luther King, Jr.* New York: Penguin, 2002, p. 118.

85. Quoted in *Reporting Civil Rights*, p. 806.

86. Quoted in Fred Powledge, *The Civil Rights Movement and the People Who Made It.* Boston: Little, Brown, 1980, p. 80.

Chapter 6:
Justice Delayed: Prosecuting Lynchers Decades Later

87. Quoted in Ginzburg, *100 Years of Lynchings*, p. 238.

88. Quoted in Errin Haines, "Lynching Anniversary Marked," *Milwaukee Journal-Sentinel*, July 26, 2005, p. 7A.

89. Quoted in *Reporting Civil Rights, Part One: American Journalism 1941–1963.* New York: Library of America, 2003.

90. Quoted in Mark Gado, "Bombingham," Court TV Crime Library. www.crimelibrary.com/terrorists_spies/terrorists/birmingham_church.

91. Quoted in Sims, *The Klan*, p. 146.

92. Quoted in Jerry Mitchell, "Online NewsHour: Pursuing the Past," Public Broadcasting System, April 18, 2002. www.pbs.org/newshour/media/clarion/mitchell.html.

93. Quoted in CBS News, "Medgar Evers Assassin Dies." www.cbsnews.com/stories/2001/01/22/national/main265984.shtml.

94. Quoted in Dray, *At the Hands of Persons Unknown*, p. 456.

95. Quoted in Carol Morello, "For Civil Rights Crusaders, Arrest Brings Relief," *Washington Post*, January 8, 2005, p. B1.

96. Quoted in Melba Newsome, "Another Ghost of Mississippi Laid to Rest," *New Crisis*, November 1998, p. 5.

97. Quoted in Lisa Hoffman, "New Office Would Open Cold Cases from Civil Rights Era," Scripps Howard News Service, September 29, 2005. www.shns.com/shns/g_index2.cfm?action=detail&pk=CIVILRIGHTS-09-29-05.

98. Quoted in Chris Dodd, "Senate Approves Talent-Dodd Unsolved Civil Rights Crime Act Bill: It Would Create New DOJ Unit to Investigate Civil Rights Cold Cases." www.dodd.senate.gov/press/Releases/05/0914.html.

99. Quoted in Hampton and Fayer, *Voices of Freedom*, p. 14.

100. *Memphis Commercial Appeal*, "Seeking Justice for Emmett Till," November 28, 2005, p. B4.

101. Quoted in Douglas O. Linder, "The Mississippi Burning Trial (U.S. vs Cecil Price et al.)," University of Missouri-Kansas City School of Law. www.law.umkc.edu/faculty/projects/ftrials/price&bowers/Account.html.

Epilogue:
The Legacy of Lynching

102. Quoted in Frank James, "Senate Apologizes for Lynchings," *Chicago Tribune*, June 13, 2005, p. A1.

103. Quoted in Ana Radelat, "Senate Apologizes for Not Enacting Anti-lynching Law," *USA Today*, June 13, 2005, p. A1.

104. Quoted in Dolores Barclay, Todd Lewan, and Allen G. Breed, "Investigation: Black Landowners Targeted," *Clarion-Ledger Mississipi News*, December 3, 2001, p. 1.

105. Quoted in "Wilkinson County Sheriff Discusses Hanging Case," *Mississippi Link*, May 27–June 1, 2004, p. A1.

106. Quoted in Faulkner Fox, "Justice in Jasper," *Texas Observer*, September 17, 1999, p. 1.

107. Quoted in Radelat, "Senate Apologizes for Not Enacting Anti-lynching Law," p. A1.

108. Quoted in Robert A. Franklin Journal, "Interview with Dr. James Cameron, Founder of America's Black Holocaust Museum." www.clt.astate.edu/rfranklin/james-camerontext.html.

For More Information

Books

Herb Boyd, *We Shall Overcome*. Naperville, IL: Sourcebooks, 2004. An excellent presentation of the civil rights era with fine pictures and two CDs with recordings of speeches and events plus narration by Ossie Davis and Ruby Dee.

James Cameron, *A Time of Terror*. Baltimore: Black Classic, 1994. The author explains what it was like to survive a lynching and his fight since then to fight racism.

Chris Crowe, *Getting Away with Murder: The True Story of the Emmett Till Case*. New York: Phyllis Fogelman, 2003. An informative book on the historic Till lynching.

Elaine Slivinski Lisandrelli, *Ida B. Wells-Barnett: Crusader Against Lynching*. Springfield, NJ: Enslow, 1998. A good biography of the anti-lynching civil rights crusader.

Ida B. Wells-Barnett, *On Lynchings: Southern Horrors, a Red Record, Mob Rule in New Orleans*. New York: Arno, 1969. Anti-lynching articles Wells-Barnett wrote.

Robert L. Zangrando, *The NAACP Crusade Against Lynching, 1909–1950*. Philadelphia: Temple University Press, 1980. The author traces the NAACP's campaign to protect blacks from lynching.

Film

American Experience: The Murder of Emmett Till, VHS. Directed by Stanley Nelson. Boston: WGBH Educational Foundation, 2003.

Web Sites

African-American Perspectives: Mob-violence and Anarchy, North and South (http://rs6.loc.gov/ammem/aap/aapmob.html). This Library of Congress Web site is informative. Its resources include printed and audio material.

American Experience: The Murder of Emmett Till (www.pbs.org/wgbh/amex/till/index.html). A Public Broadcasting System Web site with details, interviews, and photos on Till's lynching.

Black History Pages (www.blackhistory pages.com). This Web site has links to the top Web sites on lynching and other aspects of African American history.

The Civil Rights Movement (www.ecsu.ctstateu.edu/depts/edu/textbooks/civil-rights). A list of many quality Web sites on the civil rights era.

The Jim Crow Museum of Racist Memorabilia (www.ferris.edu/htmls/news/jimcrow/menu.html). This Ferris State University Web site has historical documentation and interesting graphics on the Jim Crow era.

Lynchings in America: A History Not Known by Many (www.liu.edu/cwis/cwp/library/african/2000/lynching.html). This Long Island University Web site includes historical information, photographs, and a list of books, films, and other Web sites.

Without Sanctuary (www.withoutsanctuary.org/main.html). This is the companion Web site to the book *Without Sanctuary: Lynching Photography in America.* It contains historical photographs and postcards, many of them shocking, plus information on the subject.

Index

Picture Credits

About the Author

Michael V. Uschan has written more than fifty books, including *Life of an American Soldier in Iraq,* for which he won the 2005 Council for Wisconsin Writers Juvenile Nonfiction Award. It was the second time he won the award. Mr. Uschan began his career as a writer and editor with United Press International, a wire service that provides stories to newspapers, radio, and television. Journalism is sometimes called "history in a hurry." Mr. Uschan considers writing history books a natural extension of the skills he developed in his many years as a journalist. He and his wife, Barbara, reside in the Milwaukee suburb of Franklin, Wisconsin.